Mary Berry
My Gardening Life

Mary Berry

My Gardening Life

To the gardener in my life, Kevin, who has been with us for 32 years. His answer to everything is 'no problem' and there are always stripes on the lawn.

Contents

Introduction

8

Chapter 1
My Garden Memories

12

Chapter 2
How I Garden

58

Chapter 3
My Gardening Year

96

Index 266

Acknowledgements 270

Introduction

Welcome to my garden.

This book is some jottings on my life and memories. In it, I share what gardening really means to me and how it has been a constant throughout my life. I have always found that gardens are great places for thought and finding peace. Over the years, the garden has been a great solace and a place I love to be. Whatever life may bring, being out in the garden usually makes me feel a little bit better about it.

Gardens are also good for our physical health. I'm not one for going to the gym but I find working in the garden to be a great substitute. Whenever I've been away, the first thing I do when I come home is to go straight into the garden with my dogs to do a bit of deadheading. There's always something to do.

I have been very fortunate to visit some beautiful gardens and meet the most wonderful, inspirational people too. I'll introduce some of them throughout the book and share their invaluable advice. I've learned so much from the generous gardeners I have met over the years and this has helped inform how I garden today.

One of my great joys is watching how the garden changes with the seasons. I always look forward to the crocuses popping up in the lawn in spring, the blooms of the roses through the summer, the bounty of my kitchen garden in autumn, and the neat structure of the garden in winter. Throughout the year, and throughout my life, I have always found something to enjoy in my garden.

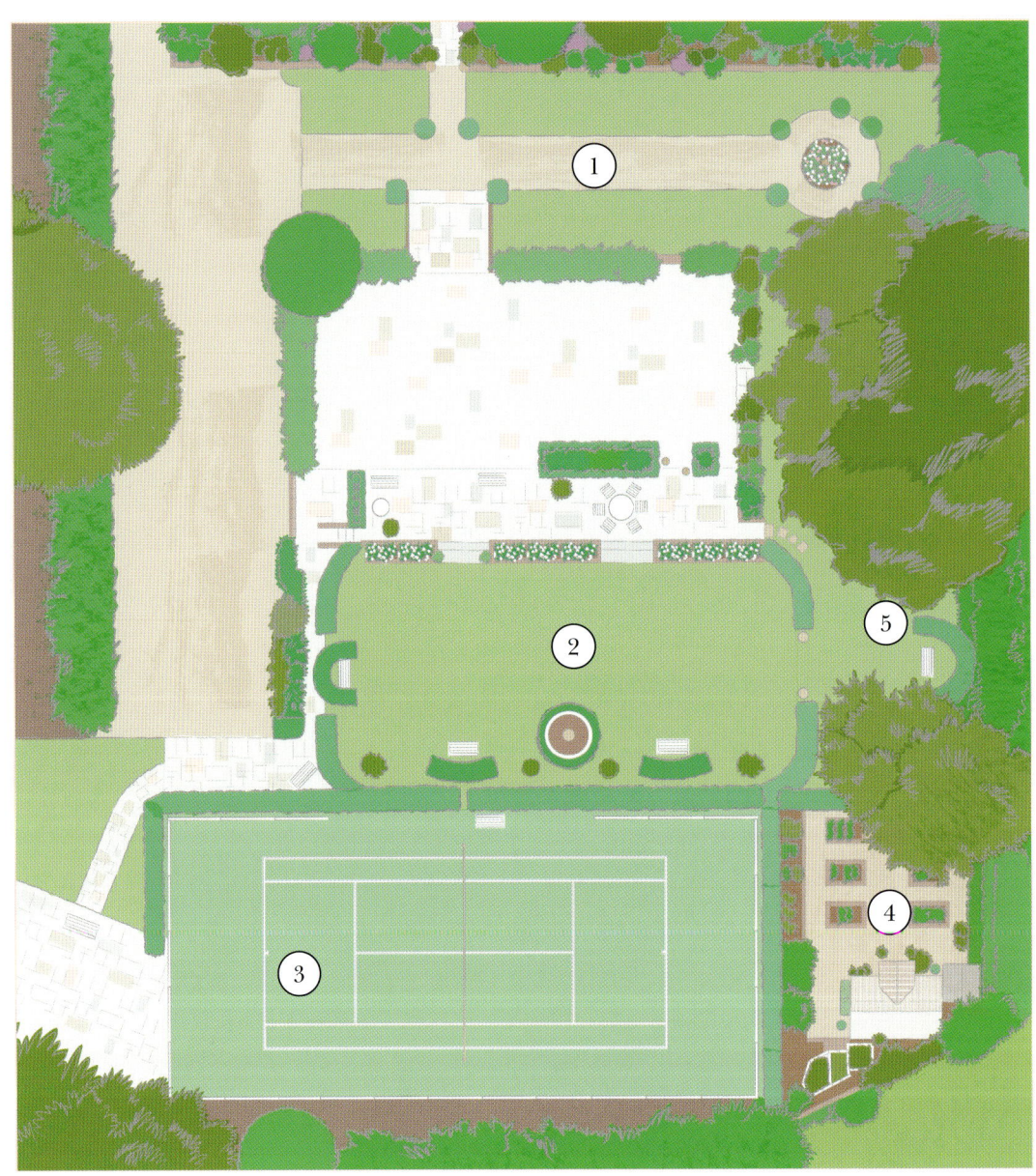

My garden plan

Here is an overview of my garden at Henley, showing how all the areas I mention throughout this book fit together. At the front, we have quite dense planting to help shield us from the road. The beds are filled with flowers and there is a gravel path dividing the lawn. We have two very large trees, one on each side of the house: an oak (left, on the picture) underplanted with ferns, and a horse chestnut (right) underplanted with hostas. At the back of the house is a terrace with garden furniture and beds of roses. This leads on to the croquet lawn and pond. Beyond the lawn is the tennis court, which is shielded by yew hedging. At the back, next to the tennis court, is the vegetable garden with raised beds and the greenhouse.

1. Front garden
2. Croquet lawn
3. Tennis court
4. Vegetable garden
5. Side lawn

My gardens over the years have been exciting experiments in discovering the plants I like best

Chapter 1
My Garden Memories

Early Memories

As a child, gathering things in the wild is my first real recollection of enjoying plants and flowers. Our family lived in a rambling house in Bath called South Lawn. It is on an unmade-up road, opposite what is now the Royal High School Bath.

Picking primroses and blackberries

When we were young, there were no theme parks or things like that and we didn't go to playgrounds. For entertainment, we played in the garden, had friends round, made dens, climbed trees, had picnics, and picked things in the wild such as primroses and blackberries. We always had dogs and would teach them to jump over logs and do tricks together. It was great fun.

We used to go primrosing in spring, and often my grandparents would be there. My father's father, Grandpa Berry, was a canon of York and was very proper and correct. He used to come on these outings wearing an overcoat and a sort of trilby-style hat. My father's mother had died when my father was two, so when Grandpa came to stay with us, he came with his housekeeper, Miss Atton.

Mum would make up a picnic, and invariably, as the weather would be cold, she'd take a Primus paraffin camping stove to make tea. This was quite a palaver as the stove had to stand on level ground, the kettle could easily tip over, and the flame frequently blew out. Fortunately, Mum had the necessary skill and always managed to make the tea in the end.

After we'd enjoyed a rock cake, we'd pick primroses and would tie them into bunches with lengths of wool. We'd put them in small vases around the house, and, most likely, I would take some to school the next day for my teacher to sweeten them up, because most of the time I was quite naughty. To this day, I still clearly remember the delicate smell of those primroses, and they remain one of my favourite flowers. They herald spring.

Later in the year, we would go blackberrying. Everybody would be given a bowl, and we'd collect the berries while Grandpa sat on a rug reading the paper as he wasn't too interested in blackberries.

Collecting art

Many years later, when we were living in Penn, Buckinghamshire, my husband, Paul, used to work for Hiram Walker in London and did quite a bit of travelling. When he was away, in between visiting clients, he used to buy pictures and prints of the country – he really was a collector. Then he decided that's what he enjoyed doing and boldly set up his own business, initially working from home.

There was a wonderful old-fashioned bakery in Penn, but it closed just before we moved there. The building continued to be used as a storage place, and the family who owned it, the Woodbridges, always promised Paul that if they ever sold up, he could have it. Sure enough, eventually they decided to sell, and Paul just walked over to see the grandfather, who owned the store, and they came to an agreement. So Paul had this as his gallery where he specialized in antiquarian books and pictures.

I couldn't resist this painting of primrose bunches. It's a reminder of my childhood and still a favourite flower.

One day, Paul asked me to visit the gallery Abbott and Holder in London to look at a watercolour they were selling. It was an image of Charlcombe Church, where we were married, and he thought it would be nice to give it to my mother. When I got there, I realized that, in fact, the watercolour wasn't Charlcombe Church after all, so unfortunately it was of no interest.

However, on the wall was a watercolour of five bunches of primroses tied up with wool. My husband had given me £100 in cash to buy the watercolour of the church, which was a lot of money at the time. Instead, I bought the picture of the primroses, which I couldn't resist. I was a bit apprehensive about what Paul's response would be, but when I showed him, he said, 'Oh, that's enchanting.'

When I told him I'd bought it to keep rather than sell, he said he loved it too and asked if I would like it for my birthday. I've put a note on the back saying 'Lucy Young'. Lucy has been working by my side for 36 years now, so when I pop my clogs, it will be hers because I know that she loves primroses too.

South Lawn

The first garden I can really remember was the one at South Lawn. I remember playing in it, because that's what we did most days, and it's where I had my first little bit of garden to myself. It's funny, but after all these years, I can remember everything about that garden.

The area at the back of the house was quite big with a central path that led down to two greenhouses and a little lawn with deckchairs where my parents used to go in summer to have a cup of coffee after lunch. One of the greenhouses contained lots of pots of deep purple cineraria for the house. The other greenhouse had pot plants and cucumbers and tomatoes in it. Just below the greenhouses was a single row of sweet peas, which I remember Mum picking each day in early July.

Top *A reluctant gardener, my father kept the garden tidy and productive in the war.* Bottom *Here I'm being led on a carthorse while staying at a farm.*

Early Memories

Wartime in Bath

My dad didn't really enjoy gardening, and Mum did no gardening at all, but because it was wartime, you really had to dig for victory. We grew enough vegetables to be self-sufficient, and I remember at the far end of the garden there were neat rows of all sorts of things such as potatoes, strawberries, raspberries, and lettuces. We didn't grow many herbs, just parsley, thyme, sage, and mint, as Mum only knew the basic ones and didn't use them that much in cooking.

Although Dad was not a keen gardener, I do remember him giving me seeds of a plant called clarkia, which grew and flowered quickly, although I was a little bit disappointed as they were not spectacular when they were in a vase. I also have memories of growing lettuce and radishes.

During the war, there was bombing in Bath for two days in 1942. In fact, my school just half a mile away was bombed, and we were told that we would have to move into nearby houses borrowed from parents for our classes. The headmistress, Miss Blackburn, asked my parents if the school could use our house, and I thought that would be excellent, as I'd just fall out of bed, go to school, and be able to nip to the kitchen to get snacks at breaktime. But, of course, it didn't work out as planned, and I had to go to a house on Lansdown Hill, quite a distance away, which I wasn't too pleased about.

When we moved into South Lawn, there was a lawned area at the front with sections cut out for roses. I remember that the roses proved to be too much work for Dad, so they were taken out and the area became simply lawn, which now seems strange as I love growing roses. There was a huge ash tree where we had a swing, and at the bottom of the front garden, a pampas grass. I can remember cutting my hands on its sharp blades and I've hated pampas ever since. I've never planted it in any of our gardens.

Even now, when I walk through a wood,
the smell of wild garlic takes me back
to the wild garlic of my childhood.

Early Memories

Along the perimeter of the front garden were iron railings hidden behind some trees. I remember one very sad day when the railings along with our huge double iron gates were taken away in lorries to be used for the war effort. At the time, we had dogs, but fortunately they were so used to staying in that we didn't need to replace the railings or gates.

Just behind where the railings used to be there was a lot of wild garlic with white flowers in spring. Even now, when I walk through a wood, that smell takes me back to the wild garlic of my childhood. Scent is very evocative of a particular memory, and I suppose that when you're a child, you have an acute sense of smell. Nobody grew wild garlic for cooking then, it was considered a weed.

The front garden also had a big, long bed of perennials with lots of flowers, and I can remember the dominant smell of phlox, lilies, and lavender in summer and the daffodils and tulips in spring. Dad was a surveyor and auctioneer, and he used to have a fellow from the sales room, Mr Barlow, come to help him in the garden. Funnily enough, Mr Barlow didn't know much about gardening either, but somehow it all seemed to happen.

Mum always picked flowers from the garden for the house, and I can still remember the smell of the various blooms she brought indoors. In summer, she would always find the coldest place, outside the back door facing north, and she put the vase there overnight to keep the flowers chilled.

In fact, I do exactly the same here. I always have flowers in the kitchen, as that is where we spend most of our time. When I take the dogs out at night, I tuck the kitchen vase under a garden table so that the flowers have a cool night and will last longer.

When I held Aga workshops at Watercroft, we had a walk-in fridge with shelving all round, and I used to put the flowers in there. It was so useful, especially if you were given a bunch of flowers and you'd already got some, you could pretend you were a florist and keep them fresh for a couple of days.

I have inherited my mum's habit of always having garden flowers in the house, and the first thing I do whenever I come home from working, or perhaps from holiday, is to dump my bags and go directly outside to see what there is to pick.

Flower girl
On Fridays, my mum used to go to do the accounts at Dad's office in Bath, and so in the school holidays, I would play in the garden at home. I don't know where my two brothers were. One day, when I was about 10 years old, I remember thinking that there were lots of spare flowers in the garden, and that if I picked them, perhaps I could sell them.

Mum always had flowers in the house, and it's a habit I have inherited.

The big gates had gone but there were two big pillars and a little curve of stubs where the iron railings used to be, so I put my buckets of flowers there. The road wasn't a very busy one, and I think I sold just two bunches. I had my little till and was so pleased that people stopped to talk to me. At the end of our road was where the Women's Royal Naval Service (WRNS) were based during the war, in what is now the Royal High School Bath, and a couple of them bought my flowers.

At one o'clock, my parents came back from the office as usual for lunch and asked me what I was doing picking and selling the flowers, as they were rather cross. After lunch, without further explanation, my father said I should go and knock on the door of Miss Jackson, who lived opposite us, and take her all the money – which amounted to two shillings and sixpence (about $12\frac{1}{2}$p) – to give to the Red Cross charity that she supported.

We knew our neighbours and I remember we'd often call in on them. Next door to us there was a dear old lady with a housekeeper, and I'd go and play canasta and snap and card games like that with her. My brothers and I made camps in our garden, and later on, I had my own pony. It was a very happy time.

Charlcombe Farm

In my early teens, while at South Lawn, I contracted polio, and after I recovered, when I was about 14, my parents moved to Charlcombe Farm, which was just about a mile away. When we arrived, there was not much of a garden as such, just a lawn with a cherry tree.

Although I wasn't involved in the garden at Charlcombe Farm, I always watched what my parents did in the garden. As with South Lawn, they had a good vegetable garden where they grew enough for us to be more or less self-sufficient. I would occasionally go out to pick a lettuce or something, but at the time, I wasn't terribly interested in plants.

There was a stream running all the way down through the fields where my dad, who was always making plans for one thing or another, decided to create a couple of watercress beds, as there was a flat area at the bottom of the field. The stream started from a natural spring, and Dad had the water tested for purity before we were allowed to grow watercress.

The two beds were essentially two big, shallow ponds, like paddling pools, that were fed by the stream. I was about 16 at the time, and even though it was freezing in the water, I would sometimes help Mum pick the watercress and put it into neat little bunches, which she'd sell to a local restaurant, called the Red House, and a greengrocer. It was quite different from the watercress you buy nowadays in supermarkets, which tends to be all in a tangle.

Dad was always creating something. His next plan was to make the ponds into a small lake with an island, so he got a farmer to dig out the earth and put a liner in. We also had outbuildings and cows. The lake is still there now.

After I left Bath High School, I went to a domestic science college, then worked as a home service advisor for the Electricity Board in Bath. I did lots of demonstrations, and I remember in some I introduced herbs into cooking.

Early Married Life

When I was 31, my husband and I got married and moved to London. Later, we moved to Penn in Buckinghamshire, where we stayed a number of years.

The marriage ceremony took place in Charlcombe Church, which is relatively small so not all our guests could fit in and a number of people had to stand outside. It was October and the church was decorated simply with white flowers and greenery. There was not a chrysanthemum in sight as my mum didn't like them, and I've inherited her dislike for them too – at least the very large, bold ones. I quite like the small spray chrysanths, and I do have them in the house in the autumn in the season where they belong.

My bouquet was simply fresh, white flowers in a modest bunch. I made the wedding cake myself and decorated it with flowers picked from the garden, which I put all the way around it along with a little silver vase of flowers in the centre. It was instant and effective and there was no need for fancy icing. Years later, we did the same for my son Tom and daughter-in-law, Sarah, but used just roses.

Tom is a tree surgeon, and for amusement when cutting the cake, he got out a little chainsaw and his safety helmet. There was a white tablecloth on the table, but underneath it was a beautiful pie crust antique table, and when I saw Thomas bringing out his saw, my heart sank because I thought it may go straight through the table. Fortunately it didn't, so that was quite a relief.

Farmer Street

Our first house as a married couple was a little terrace house in Farmer Street in Hillgate Village, West London. It was near quite a smart fish restaurant called Geales, and nobody wanted to buy

I made our wedding cake, decorating it with flowers picked from the garden.

the house because they were concerned about the cooking smells. My dad, being a surveyor, came up and looked at it for us, and he said the smells go up and down about four houses along, so actually there was no problem. We bought the house and moved in.

At the back, there was a little yard where we grew a few flowers. I was so desperately keen on this little shady patch of a garden that I used to think I couldn't go away at weekends. It was small, so small that we didn't even have a table and chairs, and because it was shady, it was difficult to grow things well, but it was so good to have an outdoor space. We spent a lot of time out there with a cup of tea, coffee, or a glass of wine.

We all know how important gardening is for our health and wellbeing. Being in nature is so good for us, and I've always found that spending time outdoors in the fresh air helps all worries go away – it is the best health cure ever.

Gaining gardening knowledge
At the time, I had no confidence in my gardening abilities at all, but I was always asking, watching, and reading. We didn't have television when we began living there, but I did read lots of gardening books and seed/plant catalogues.

At weekends, my husband, Paul, and I often used to stay with my very best friend, Penny Block, at her family home in Little Gaddesden in Hertfordshire. Penny was a good gardener but her mother, Mum Block, was an amazing gardener. I'd spend time with her in the garden, and she taught me a lot about the things she grew and used to give me plants.

One day, I remember her pulling up the Michaelmas daisies – or asters as they're now called – and I asked if I could have them. She said that, in fact, I wouldn't like them because they get rust and it would go to other plants, which is why she was pulling them out, so I took her advice. Of course, now I do have asters because there are newer varieties that don't get rust, and this lovely plant is a huge joy to me in late summer and autumn.

If I wanted to talk to Mum Block, I could always find her in the garden, and she would hardly lift her head as she talked. She taught me all about roses, especially her techniques for pruning. She was a very harsh pruner and would always say, cut out anything thinner than a pencil, and that advice has stuck. I remember her taking climbing roses down off the wall, laying them on the ground, trimming them, then putting them back up again. I think of Mum Block from time to time and am grateful for all her guidance. She had a great influence on my life.

Her daughter Penny was also a terrific gardener, and we used to go and look at National Garden Scheme (NGS) gardens together at weekends. Sadly, Penny has died, but I enjoy gardening banter with her sister, Hilly. It's in the family, and Hilly comes to stay and we visit gardens together.

It took me a while to get the hang of what would grow at Farmer Street. I made so many mistakes there because I wanted to grow a bit of everything and kept wondering why things kept dying. Nothing grew because it really was in total shade. Now, of course, I realize that it is very, very important to choose the right plants for your garden's conditions. I know much more about shade-loving plants and could say exactly what I should have put in.

One of my successes was the hanging baskets we had either side of the front door at Farmer Street. I'm not keen on hanging baskets now that I live in the countryside, but I was so proud of the ones I had in London. I used to put in lots of annuals, quite close together, and they thrived.

They were on the sunny side of the house, and I developed a little routine for watering them. In those days, we had milk delivered, and every morning when I took the empty bottles out, I would fill them with water and put half in each of the hanging baskets. That was the reason they always looked beautiful. I learned that if you let hanging baskets get too dry, they will not absorb water and it will just run off. Some people suggest taking them down and immersing them in water, but I never had to do that, and they were always brilliant. That was when I really got into gardening.

My Garden Memories

The Red House

After three years at Farmer Street, we moved to the Red House in Penn, Buckinghamshire, as we wanted more space and a proper garden for our two boys to play in (Annabel was born a few years after we moved). It was at the Red House that I realized the importance of sun, shade, and soil, and that you can't garden successfully if you have to battle with plants that aren't right for your conditions.

While visiting a garden that was open for the NGS, I remember admiring a large, deciduous shrub with beautiful, glossy, green leaves and large, white flowers called *Eucryphia glutinosa*. I'd read somewhere to always buy in threes or fives, so I bought three of these shrubs as we now had quite a sizeable garden. However, we had chalk on clay in Penn, and that particular shrub definitely does best on an acid soil. They all died and so I learned my lesson.

The garden at the Red House was about an acre (0.4 hectare), three-quarters of it around the house and a quarter-acre field adjacent to it. Much of the garden at the Red House was given over to grass, which was ideal for the boys to play rugby on.

There were a few perennial borders and a lovely weeping beech with branches that came well down to the ground, which the children would hide in. In one section of the garden, which strangely had acid soil, there were lots of camellias. We had a small, lean-to greenhouse where I used to put any pot plants that were past their best, with the hope they might come again. I also grew tomatoes in there.

A children's playground

At the time, the garden was mainly used as a playground for the children – it was a rugby field, a football pitch, a cricket pitch, and a place for hide and seek and children's parties. In those days, we

Top *The Red House, which gave us more space to enjoy the garden as a family.*
Bottom *In the kitchen with my three children, Tom, Annabel, and William.*

made the entertainment ourselves. The children all loved the freedom of being outside walking with the dogs, and we'd collect different leaves, sticks, and stones, things like that. When we got home, we'd spread them out on the kitchen table and identify exactly what they were. We'd also find footprints and get the children to work out what wild animal they belonged to. A walk was always about discovering what was in nature; it was great fun.

Childhood antics and budding gardeners
I can remember it was William's fifth birthday, and we were playing grandmother's footsteps on the playing lawn with all the children and mothers there. I looked up to the top of the house, a tall, three-storey, red-brick building, and there, walking along the ridge, was Thomas, who was about seven years old. I said to the mothers, 'Please don't look up and please don't tell the children.' I think he was waiting for us to wave at him or something. After some time had passed, he came down safely for tea, but he was obviously being rebellious because it was his younger brother's birthday!

When he was about 15 years old, William became very keen on gardening and had a bedroom full of houseplants. He used to help me around the garden, whereas Thomas, our eldest son, couldn't be bothered. Thomas now has a tree surgery business and loves the great outdoors. Our daughter, Annabel, didn't get involved either at the time but is now a very keen gardener and is learning fast, so evidently some things stuck.

We would often visit my parents' house in Bath, and the children loved the lake or the pond, whatever you like to call it, that my father had built. He put some sand and gravel at one end so that we had our own beach, and we used to have picnics there with our children and friends' children.

One Christmas, I remember we said that whoever could swim around the island would get £1. Everyone refused to do it apart from our son William, who was about 16 at the time and a good swimmer. On Christmas Day, he was true to his word and swam all the way around so got his £1. None of the others dared to do it!

Finding time to garden
It was while living in the Red House that we travelled to London by train every day for work. At that stage, I had two jobs: I was working on magazines doing cookery features, and I also worked for Benson's PR company running a test kitchen developing recipes for all sorts of clients. My husband worked for Hiram Walker, and we would go to London together and come back on the same train. I used to get the seed catalogues from Suttons and Thompson & Morgan and would sit on the train dreaming of all the wonderful things I'd grow. I have to say, I didn't have great success with many of them but I loved the catalogues.

While living at the Red House, although I was beginning to really enjoy gardening, I didn't have much spare time to do it. I always tried to have flowers to pick for the house and we did grow a few vegetables, although not terribly successfully. My book agent, Felicity Bryan, said, wisely, not to worry because when the children didn't need me as much then I'd have more time for gardening. Felicity was an excellent gardener herself and was, for a time, the gardening expert for the *Evening Standard*.

Actually, it was Delia Smith who introduced me to Felicity. Delia came to stay with us with her husband, Michael, and I know that there is an unwritten rule that you should never discuss money, sex, or religion, but of course we did discuss work and money! Delia suggested that it would be good for me to have an agent, and three days later, I had a postcard from Felicity, so I began working with her. It was so kind of Delia and we've remained friends ever since. I have always admired her.

Recent Decades

After about 15 years at the Red House, we moved a stone's throw away to Watercroft, also in Penn, as we wanted even more garden. In fact, we swapped houses with our neighbour, Lady Heath, when her husband, Sir Barrie Heath, died. The garden at Watercroft extended to 3.5 acres (1.4 hectares), and it featured a narrow pathway running down the centre with rose arches and perennial planting on either side.

Watercroft

The first thing that we did was to widen the pathway beneath the rose arches so that two people could walk side by side, and moved all of the perennials to the border around the perimeter of the garden and replaced them with my favourite roses. We had a number of different roses in little groups, including *Rosa* 'Garnette Rose', 'The Fairy', 'Peace', and 'Rosemary Harkness', which did well. It was a great way of seeing which ones I liked best. The way they were arranged was very higgledy piggledy but there was a huge batch of 'The Fairy' in the middle, which I loved.

There was a three-sided courtyard, and where it opened out onto the main garden, I grew the 'Chandos Beauty' rose. Everyone used to admire it. We bought them from Harkness Roses in Hitchin, Hertfordshire, which is not far away from us. In fact, we went to their nursery and met Philip Harkness, and he told us that all of their roses are grown on site, and they certainly seem very healthy.

Harkness publishes a catalogue, which I think is very good for someone like me who doesn't know too much about roses as they give them a star system, with marks out of 10 for general health, foliage, and scent. The catalogue makes it easier to choose, and 'Chandos Beauty' had full marks for both categories – it really is a brilliant rose.

The garden at Watercroft featured an attractive, natural, clay-based pond.

Slugs and soil
It was really quite striking where we'd made the path wider, planted the arches with roses, and flanked each side of the path with *Nepeta* x *faassenii* – a dwarf variety of catmint. Of course, the *Nepeta* died down and we cut it back before the winter, but then one year, it didn't come back. So I got on my hands and knees, carefully drew some of the soil aside, and saw that every little shoot had been eaten by slugs. I've seen exactly the same thing happen with delphiniums. While it's not advised these days, I did put a few slug pellets down and, as we had a gravel drive, I used to take buckets of gravel and put it along where the *Nepeta* was growing. Slugs don't like gravel, so it helped and eventually the shoots came through.

Not long after moving in, we sent samples of soil off to the RHS to be tested so that we would know exactly what we were dealing with. It transpired that it was mostly chalk on clay. I'd always recommend testing the soil of a garden that is new to you as it helps you know what you are dealing with from the outset.

At one point, our sons, William and Thomas, planted Christmas trees in our field at the bottom of the property. It was very damp and it turned out to be perfect for Christmas trees. Years later, Thomas and his new wife dressed up in Father Christmas outfits, sold the trees from the car park opposite the church, and gave a donation to the church. They had hot drinks and mince pies and had a great time.

Shaping the garden
When we moved into Watercroft, there was not much room to leave cars in the drive, so we decided to create a car park. The original vegetable garden was huge – far too big for our needs – so we used that area for a decent-sized car park, enclosing it with a beech hedge. It meant that when I did our Aga workshops, there was plenty of space for cars. We always had lots of friends and visitors come too.

I love climbers and we had a passion flower growing up one of the walls, along with a *Clematis* 'Hagley Hybrid', which grows well in shade. I always cut it down at the end of the season to around 6 inches (15 centimetres) and it would come back again in spring no problem.

Creating a pond
One of my great joys in that garden was the pond. On the ridge in Penn as you drive through, all the original houses had natural ponds with a clay base, and after a few years at Watercroft, we decided to make our pond bigger. Our son Tom is very practical, so we knew he could help us create one.

We hired a digger and took out soil alongside the pond to make it much bigger and created a small island in the middle. It all worked really well, and it was so exciting to dig out a section and suddenly see spring water bubbling through the clay.

The little island was so peaceful and became a haven for our dearly cherished resident ducks. They were well looked after every day and they used the island as a retreat at night so that Mr Fox didn't get them. One of our ducks, Lonely, was very special, so named because she was often on her own without a partner. But each year she gave us the joy of ducklings, so I guess she was never that lonely!

I was greatly inspired by a visit to Longstock Park Water Garden, part of John Lewis's Leckford Estate in Hampshire. I was there doing cookery demonstrations for a Waitrose customer day. Mike Stone, who was in charge of the gardens at the time and had helped create them, kindly showed us around. I thought both the layout and the planting were brilliant.

Mike mentioned that he was due to retire, so I took his phone number, and the following January, after he'd left, I contacted him to ask if he'd help guide us with the planting and maintenance of our pond. At the time, we opened the garden for the NGS, and the pond was quite an important feature. Fortunately, Mike agreed to help and he was absolutely delightful. He suggested how to structure it, what plants to have, what not to have, and also helped us to put all the plants in.

On the whole, I wanted plants around the margin that weren't too difficult to maintain and that would establish themselves quickly. Very wisely, he advised us to take out all of the bulrushes and the yellow flag iris (*Iris pseudacorus*) because they were just spreading into the pond, so we did just that. Instead, we planted lots of marginals around the pond, including crimson flag lilies (*Hesperantha coccinea*), lots of primulas, astilbes, rodgersias, various irises, umbrella plants (*Darmera peltata*), and gunneras.

It's interesting how times change, as now we are now told not to plant gunnera as it's considered invasive. In fact, we found that while it got established and looked very attractive, it certainly didn't overpower the pond. Mike encouraged me to water everything really well in the first year to get plants established.

Every morning we'd look out onto the pond, which was serene and restful, a great way to start the day.

In the middle of the pond, we had the island as a haven for the ducks. Unfortunately, however, the planting wasn't terribly successful – talk about mistakes! We had a weeping willow, but that got rather too big, along with lots of ferns and primulas, but those all died as I couldn't get over to the island to water them without a lot of fuss. I realized then just how important it is when you're putting in new plants to not only soak the roots beforehand but, over the course of the first and even the second year, to water regularly to help things really get established.

We had loads of wildlife in the garden, and at one point, there were always some carp and goldfish in the pond. Friends gave us goldfish from the Penn Charter Fair that their children had won. They arrived in plastic bags with string handles and we would pop them in the pond. They would be so happy and grow and thrive, although I don't think this happens at fairs now!

Overall, the whole thing was such a success. The pond faced the front of the house and was overlooked by the drawing room and our bedroom, which had a balcony. Every morning we'd look out onto the pond, which was simply wonderful. Mike Stone was given an award by the RHS in recognition of his services to horticulture, yet he was so modest. Sadly, he has since died, but he did see the completed pond.

Herbs, vegetables, and flowers
We also had expert advice for the herb garden, which we built near the house. It was laid out with bricks in a pattern and little paths running through it, and all the herbs were edible as I'm not really into medicinal herbs. We grew perennial culinary herbs along with basil and dill grown as annuals in the main garden.

Every year a partridge would come and lay its eggs under a large sage plant, and I used to watch and keep the dogs away. It was so exciting knowing that they were there. We'd see the broken shells and know the eggs had hatched, but sadly, the partridges always swept off in the night and we never saw the youngsters.

Having done away with the big original vegetable garden, we built a more modest-sized one with brick pathways and box edging. Unfortunately, the box suffered from blight, so we replaced it with *Veronica rigidula*. It was fairly successful, but in hindsight, I would have planted yew.

With vegetable growing, one of the biggest lessons I have learned is to simply grow what we as a family like to eat. I also avoid planting things that are relatively cheap to buy, such as potatoes and onions. We always had runner beans, and I found an expert to make an arch out of hazel poles, which looked attractive and made it quite easy to pick them.

Inspired by gardener Sarah Raven, we built a picking bed. First, we improved the soil and then planted all the flowers I liked to have in the house. In the autumn, we used to have lots of dahlias, and I planted only those that looked good in a vase, including lots of the single ones, which I particularly like. I never have the really big-headed ones as I'm not keen on those. There were lots of alstroemerias, which are so good for picking as they last extremely

well in the vase. I tried to grow larkspur, which I love, but never had much success with it. Delphiniums are lovely too but are also difficult to grow as they suffer from slugs, although with care they can be successful. I used slug pellets then at the base of the plants, but covered them with heaps of gravel so that they are out of the way of birds.

We bought lots of delphiniums from the specialist grower Blackmore & Langdon's near Bristol, and one of my favourites is 'Molly Buchanan', a glorious deep blue with a dark, almost black eye at the centre. It is named after my aunt, my mum's sister. We had lots of bulbs too, including scented narcissus, such as the ivory-coloured 'Silver Chimes,' and of course, what's good about bulbs is that they tend to come up every year.

Our flower meadow

We had a meadow that had been planted by our predecessors, Sir Barrie and Lady Heath, with a seed mix, Cricklade North Meadow Mixture (from Emorsgate Seeds). It was lovely, full of different grasses and a few oxeye daisies. The meadow was far too big for us to put in lots of bulbs, so wasn't like the one at Highgrove that Prince Charles, as he then was, planted, which has lots of dark tulips.

In those days, I didn't know about planting yellow rattle (*Rhinanthus minor*), which reduces the vigour and competitiveness of grasses. Had I taken out sections and put yellow rattle in, then most likely I would have had more interesting things grow.

My husband had the brilliant idea of mowing pathways through the meadow, so we had one path cut that went down it and another across the middle so that they formed a cross, and then a third one that went all the way around it. At the top and bottom of the meadow, either side of the mown path, we planted the wilder-looking white rugosa roses. It was lovely to walk through the meadow along these paths, and they made it much easier to mow the whole thing, which we did once a year in about September.

Originally, the pathways in the vegetable garden were lined with box, but later we replaced it with Veronica rigidula.

When we opened the garden for the NGS, generally in July, as well as adult visitors, we'd often get lots of children come along too, and they loved racing along the pathways. They would run around the corners and hide behind the long grass so that no one could see them.

The garden had two walls: one on the roadside and the other on the east side. Along these were climbing roses and an evergreen *Magnolia grandiflora* 'Exmouth', which we pruned each year as it grows quickly.

Gardening inspiration

While living at Watercroft, I used to go with a local gardening group to see interesting gardens. The group was run by Margaret Thorpe, a keen gardener who had a wealth of knowledge. When she started teaching classes in the village hall at Burnham, not far from us, I started to go there with my great friend Claire White, who is now an excellent practical gardener with a great eye for design.

Margaret was absolutely brilliant, and I learned so much from her. When she suggested that we should do some practical work, I asked her to come to Watercroft. She taught me about pruning various shrubs, such as forsythia, *Philadelphus*, and deutzia, which you prune after flowering.

One day, having visited Sutton Place in Surrey and admired their wonderful hedges and topiary, I said to my husband, Paul, 'You know where that old tennis court is, halfway down the garden, where the grass doesn't grow very well? Why don't we just hedge it in? We could have a circle in the middle with a path going down?' He replied, 'Well, don't just talk about it, grasp the nettle and do it.'

He gave me some graph paper, so I drew up a plan. We put in yew, a gravel path, and a few steps going down into it with two urns. Later we planted a yew hedge behind the urns and built steps down to the wild meadow. It worked well and added another area of interest.

Seeking advice

We decided that we had room to have a small arboretum. It sounds grand but really it was just a collection of interesting trees. I'm a great one for getting advice, so we went to Hillier Garden Centre

We bought these urns in memory of Paul's boss at Hiram Walker, who'd bequeathed Paul a sum of money. When we moved to Henley, we took them with us.

and got one of their experts to help us choose trees. I took samples of the soil and pictures of the area. We paid £25, but that was 40 years ago. We had all sorts of trees that I wouldn't have thought of, and it's absolutely worth spending money to get good advice, particularly when you're putting in long-term plants such as trees.

We planted a gingko, but it was too shaded by another big tree and it never did well. I learned that gingko grows better in the open, but you learn by your mistakes.

Watercroft really was a lovely garden, and we were very fortunate.

Our gardener for 32 years has been Kevin Pryce. When he started with us, he was a very keen young man, and over the years, has taken all his horticultural exams. He's a great friend and hugely knowledgeable, and I always ask for his advice before I do anything.

At Watercroft, he came to us for two days a week and now he comes once a week, always on Thursdays at 7:30am, and for me, Thursday is always my favourite day of the week. In this book, where I say 'I', if it's anything tricky, anything to do with digging, or any task that needs to be done during the cold winter weather, it's not me that does it, it's Kevin!

Watercroft really was a lovely garden, and we were very fortunate. I learned so much about gardening and the plants I liked best there. It was really all a great experiment. One of the joys of visiting other gardens, particularly through the NGS, is that it gives one a wealth of ideas. We had plenty of room, so if I was inspired by one of my many trips to see open gardens with the NGS, I could usually buy something at the plant sales area, which was thrilling. If you are lucky, a plant that you admire in the garden is there to take home.

My Aga cookery days
It was while we were at Watercroft that I started the Aga cookery days. Our son William had sadly died, and I had not the yen to

travel to London, so decided to run courses instead. Why did I do Aga days? Well, because I had had an Aga cooker all my married life since we'd moved out to the country. I'd been commissioned to write *The Aga Book*, so I certainly knew what I was talking about. I found that many people didn't understand the principles of the Aga and so I decided that I would teach. After all, I already had a teaching qualification and sharing my knowledge is what I really love doing.

Around 20 people would come on the courses, once or sometimes twice a week, and I would teach them the Aga technique. They would usually arrive at 10am and we'd show them how to make and cook 10 or so dishes. Lucy Young had just joined me and together we set about it – I demonstrated in the morning, and Lucy demonstrated in the afternoon.

To launch it, I invited the journalists that I knew from my magazine days in London, including Katie Stewart, Philippa Davenport, and many more, to join in a trial day we'd created for them. They all came down by train, and some of my kind girlfriends cleaned their cars and went to collect them from the station. It was exciting, but when the door opened and they all walked in, I remember thinking, 'What have I let myself in for?'

I showed them the principles of cooking with an Aga and all the tricks of the trade. We gave them a jolly good lunch and off they went back to London. Then I thought, 'Well, that was interesting', and the following week in various newspapers and magazines, including the *Evening Standard*, the *Times*, and the *Telegraph*, details suddenly appeared about our Aga workshops. Up to that point, we hadn't booked any more, and I said to Lucy, 'Let's just book two days in three weeks' time', and immediately people booked. We never did any advertising, and for 16 years we were always full.

Penny Block, my great gardening friend, was very good at maths, so we thought we'd have a little Aga shop in the hall with all the equipment that I thought was very good. Before we'd built our own parking, people used to come and put their cars in the church car park opposite, and we bought 20 director's chairs because we thought they'd be nice and comfy and would fit in the kitchen. I put a mobile demonstration table with drawers just in front of the Aga and we were all set. We made a second big kitchen in what was called the Gun Room when the Heaths lived at Watercroft, and this became the prep kitchen where everything was prepared and washed up.

> *Everyone who came along was delightful, and when they arrived, we would give them coffee and homemade shortbread cooked in the Aga.*

People used to arrive at 10am and immediately wanted to bag seats, and having been on holidays where people bag seats by the pool, I thought we're having none of that here. So I said to people there is to be no bagging of seats, just go and have coffee and you can all see the demonstrations wherever you sit. So then people learned the rules and stopped coming terribly early to get what they imagined was the best seat.

When they arrived, we would give them coffee and homemade shortbread cooked in the Aga, then they would sit down and watch the demonstrations. We decided right from the very beginning that we would make it a luxury day out and that they could go all over the house. I was adamant that there would be no restrictions, because if you're opening up your home, then people should be allowed to see your home. I think people appreciated that. Only our bedroom was out of bounds.

People used to ask, 'But don't you have things taken?' but we never did. Everyone who came along was delightful, just like the people for the NGS. Often, the children were around, and my husband was very tolerant. He had the gallery in the village, and he left at 9am before anyone had arrived and then he didn't come back until after 3:30pm, when everyone had gone.

As well as tasting the 10 or so dishes in the demonstration, we also made them a separate first-rate lunch and they could drink as much wine as they wanted, but they were always sensible. For each course, we'd test recipes beforehand. Often, people would come with a family member such as their daughter or son, or with a best friend or neighbour, and once they'd been to one Aga day, they often wanted to come to another.

We'd have easy days and trickier days and always used homegrown veg and fresh herbs. It really became a place to develop great friendships. The course ran over two days, so 12 hours in total, and at lunchtime people loved going out into the garden. If they wanted to take cuttings, they were very welcome to do so. If it was a lovely day, they'd often go right down the bottom of the garden to the meadow. I think people enjoyed the freedom.

Apart from courses held in showrooms and such, there were no other courses like ours at the time. Being held in a home was really something quite different. Other cooks began running cookery schools too, but the difference with ours is that we never got anyone else apart from Lucy and myself to do it. That said, there was one day when I was ill and really out for the count, so at short notice we called Dawn Roads, head home economist for Aga, a great expert and dear friend, to step in.

I'm terrible at people's names, so we decided that as soon as they arrived, my friend Penny would make sure that everyone had a sticker with their name on along with a little star if they'd been to us before. So when they came into the kitchen where I would be doing last-minute preparations, I would say things like, 'Oh, good morning, Jane, how lovely to see you again.' It was our secret code so people would think I had a fantastic memory, it really made me laugh.

People travelled from all over the country, and I remember we used to have a lot from Scotland and Yorkshire. They would stay overnight at a local B&B, and we took on the responsibility of finding places where people could stay nearby – often it was with our neighbours.

We wanted to offer people the very best, a real treat, a day out, and it worked out really well but it wasn't cheap. We gave everyone a nice folder with typed copies of all the recipes so that they could try them out at home. We usually ran the courses on Tuesday and Wednesday each week and employed two local ladies to help in the background, and they enjoyed it all too.

Over the 16 years we ran these courses, we taught around 14,000 people in total, many of whom came through the door as repeat visitors. It was really good fun, and people had lots of very happy days out. And what's more, Lucy and I enjoyed teaching the skills that we had.

Gardening afternoons
After we'd been running these courses for a few years, I thought it would be good to offer gardening afternoons too, so I contacted Sarah Raven, whom I greatly admired, and she agreed to come up from Sussex to teach gardening. I'd read her first book, called *The Cutting Garden*, which was excellent.

We had a big glasshouse where we put a large table for Sarah to demonstrate from. She would arrive at 8am and we'd talk gardening before the day began. It was a great relief, having cooked all morning, to listen to Sarah talk in the afternoon, and I would sit there rapt with my notebook. She would invariably bring plants to show those who had had a morning of Aga cookery, and would share her know-how and tips for growing cut flowers. Sarah really was brilliant, and everyone absolutely loved her. I learned a huge amount and I realized that Aga owners are often keen gardeners too.

Not long afterwards, Sarah Raven invited me to go down to her garden at Perch Hill and do cookery days for her groups. I'd stay overnight beforehand at Sissinghurst, the family home of her husband, Adam, before they moved to Perch Hill. It was very interesting to spend time there. Sarah is incredibly bright, has a great sense of fun, and is very good at sharing the important things. It was Sarah who taught me that if you plant tulips deeper, they are more likely to come back the following year.

We also had the garden designer James Bolton to teach on half days, and since then, I have been enjoying visits to private gardens with delicious lunches, which James organizes.

Henley-on-Thames

After just under 30 years at Watercroft, we moved to our current house in Henley-on-Thames, Oxfordshire, which is a more modest and manageable Georgian house with a smaller garden. In fact, we bought the house in 2017, but we didn't move into it until 2019 as we made huge alterations to it. Each year, I plan a little scheme to improve the garden.

Making changes
When we arrived, there was very little of interest in the garden, and I was delighted that things needed to be done. I thought it would be good to get some help from someone to design parts of it. I've always admired garden designer Bunny Guinness's approach and I'd met her, so I asked her if she'd please come and help. I explained that we wanted a garden that, once established, was relatively easy to maintain, and that the main problem was that the view from the house was of the tennis court just 20 to 30 yards (18 to 27 metres) away. I also wanted to always have something to pick for the house.

I have no training, and I would have made a real mess trying to do it on my own. I always think that if you feel you need help, choose someone who makes the sort of gardens and planting you like, find out how much they would charge, and talk things through in detail to make sure they understand what you want. Designers will invariably come up with ideas we would never think of. I'm very grateful to Bunny for all of the advice that she gave me.

When we arrived here, we extended the house with a new conservatory off the kitchen. We were never too keen on glass conservatories but loved the feeling of light, so we chose not to have glass for the roof as it gets too hot. It's more like a room with a pitched roof and windows on all sides with views over the garden.

Running along the back of the house was a very narrow terrace, and Bunny widened this so that we could have a decent-sized table and chairs and take a trolley of food across it. She'd quickly realized that we loved spending time outside as a family.

Q & A
Bunny Guinness

I have always admired Bunny's work as a writer and landscape architect, and she helped me design our new garden, listening, understanding, and creating something that was right for us. I've taken so much of Bunny's advice, such as using bottomless pots, growing plenty of yew hedging, and growing *Salvia* 'Amistad', which we take cuttings of each year.

What's your approach to a planting plan?

When I'm planning a border, I start off with deciding on the structural plants. These may be a framework of low hedging – often yew (*Taxus*) now instead of box (*Buxus*). Yew can be kept to 16 by 16 inches (40 by 40 centimetres) with no problem for many, many years. The low hedging might form a pattern through the planting of diamonds, serpentines, or ellipses.

There might be small, multistem trees – such as medlars (*Mespilus*), hawthorns (*Crataegus*), or quince (*Cydonia oblonga*) – repeated within the border for more structure, or big bobbles or topiary of yew, holly (*Ilex*), *Osmanthus*, or similar. I also often use planted obelisks to add more all-round interest and to punctuate the border.

These structural plants may contribute 30 to 40 per cent of the planting and then I will fill in with the more colourful plants. Roses are usually on my list – good, healthy, long-flowering shrub roses that tolerate non-perfect conditions, such as *Rosa* 'James L. Austin', 'Emma Bridgewater', or 'Sally Holmes'.

Lower plants such as *Nepeta grandiflora* 'Summer Magic' (which does not flop and flowers far longer than most catmints), *Salvia* 'Nachtvlinder',

Daphne odora 'Aureomarginata', and *Stachys byzantina* 'Big Ears' are plants I regularly use to fill the spaces between the more structural plants.

I pop in a few fast-growing fillers for the early years, which can be pulled out as the slower plants take hold, such as *Matthiola incana* 'Alba', perennial wallflowers, and/or *Hesperis matrionalis* (sweet rocket). Tulips, *Eremurus* (foxtail lilies), *Salvia* 'Amistad', and *Canna* x *ehemanii* are fun to dot through to add high spots. I love many umbelliferas too. Perhaps the most useful perennial one is *Molopospermum peloponnesiacum* (striped hemlock).

When designing a garden, what are your top priorities?

We spend the day with the client on site with an accurate survey. Having taken onboard all their problems and ideas we come up with a design, sketching proposals over the survey. Watching and hearing the clients' reactions, we then refine the designs accordingly, so at the end of the day we arrive at a design that both the client and I think is the best possible outcome. Another day or two are spent drawing it up accurately.

Wherever possible, we try to arrange parking areas so cars are hidden, and put planting in the front of the house to emphasize the good architectural parts and deflect from less attractive ones.

Trees in baseless pots are fabulous for adding cohesion or screening to a building. Then it's a question of dividing the garden up into beautiful, usable spaces that relate to the house – I think this is the bit many struggle with. Getting the maintenance requirements of the finished garden to suit the clients is vital.

What are your tips for growing plants in large container pots?

I use a lot of baseless pots. Our YouTube video on these has had over a million hits, and lots of people are doing it now with great results. The compost in a pot slowly decomposes, so it has no capacity to hold air and does not drain well or provide a healthy growing medium. By removing the base of the pot and putting a depth of 16 inches (40 centimetres) of soil under the pot base, the plant will quickly be able to access the soil below ground. It works with everything!

What is your favourite gardening tool or piece of kit?

A great pair of gardening gloves: thick, winter ones and thin, summer ones. I get a box wholesale so I am never without. With the internet, most people can access wholesale and it's usually far better quality and far less expensive!

Opposite *The garden in Henley before work began. The view from the back of the house led straight up a crazy-paving path to the tennis court. Note there is no hedge!*

Above *We planted yew hedging to screen the tennis court and put a discreet entrance off to one side. We added a pond (see page 53) and brought the topiary spirals from our previous garden, Watercroft.*

The main garden proper is to the rear of the house and, as much as I love tennis, the eyesore for me was the view of the tennis court, which was in full view behind the lawn. We decided to screen it with yew hedging. It's always good and more economical to buy little plants and watch them grow tall, but I thought if we did that then I'd be about 120 before they reached a decent hedge height. So as a great extravagance, we bought some relatively mature plants about 4 feet (1.2 metres) tall and put in a leaky hose to make sure they didn't dry out. They've grown really well, and after about four years, we couldn't see the tennis court – just a little of the netting – so we're getting there.

Originally, we had stepping stones to the gate of the tennis court, but we didn't want to see the entrance, so Bunny made a little block of hedge that sits in front to hide it, and we just walk behind that. It really was such a good idea.

Then we thought we'd have two little blocks of hedging to the left, to separate off the lawn, which we use as a place to display a couple of large urns that we already had. The story behind these lovely urns is that when Paul's boss at Hiram Walker died, he left Paul a sum of money, and we bought these urns in his memory (see page 39). When we moved to Henley, we made sure to bring them.

Bunny also put in two semicircles of yew hedging at opposite ends of the lawn to wrap around a couple of benches that we'd brought from our previous garden. I'd visited the Laskett, Sir Roy Strong's garden in Herefordshire, and he had yew hedges with sloping shoulders on them, which I thought looked terribly smart. We did it at the last house and we're in the process of doing it here too because it's lovely.

Of course, all the hedges we've put in have made a tremendous difference. They bring year-round structure and a lovely sense of enclosure. Occasionally, we set up a long table for dining with a large group of friends, and the lawned area is perfect for this.

In summer, we sometimes set up a long table on the lawn in the shade of the chestnut tree. It's the perfect spot for lunch with a large group.

Penny's pond

When my great friend Penny Tetley died, she kindly left me a small legacy, and I thought I would do something in the garden with it. So I copied a circular pond I'd seen in Alan Titchmarsh's wonderful garden and had it built on the lawn just in front of the hedging, flanked by two topiary spirals in pots. In the middle of the pond, I chose to put a big stone sphere that had irrigation through the centre so that water trickles down. The birds love it, and it means that I don't need to have a bird bath.

Initially, however, the sphere was stark white, and the pond itself was white. It all looked awful, and I kept wondering what on earth I had done wrong. I could see my husband thought it was a mistake too, but he was trying not to upset me because I was doing it in memory of Penny. Eventually, we decided to put a little yew hedge around it, and within a few years, the whole thing weathered and mellowed, and now it looks as though it's been there forever and really is lovely.

The vegetable garden

In the top left-hand corner of the garden, we have a modest-sized vegetable garden with six raised beds made of brick that I can sit on, if need be, along with a really beautiful Alitex greenhouse. A great plus of these greenhouses is that they do not need regular maintenance and painting.

You enter the garden through an archway over which we've grown the evergreen climber star jasmine (*Trachelospermum jasminoides*), which has small, beautifully scented, white flowers. In its first year, it got hit by the frost, so for a few years, we covered it with fleece over winter, and now it's really got going and has toughened up. It has such a lovely scent.

The vegetable garden leads to a narrow area at the back of the garden, running behind the tennis court, which is hidden away so

We created this circular pond with a stone sphere in memory of my dear friend Penny Tetley. It is flanked by two topiary spirals (see also page 49).

the idea is for the dogs to do their thing there. My husband goes each morning with a metal beach spade to clear up after them. The pathway is covered in woodchips, which my son Tom, who's a tree surgeon, gave us. In the long, narrow beds alongside, I grow a few eucalyptuses, forsythia, winter-flowering honeysuckle, and various other shrubs that I cut for foliage. You can walk all the way around the back and sides of the tennis court back to the house.

One of the things I really love in a garden is estate fencing. Initially, I thought that there was no place for it here, but then I realized it would be perfect as a way of separating the front and back areas of the garden and keeping the dogs absolutely safe when the main front gate is open. So we ended up putting some in along with a nice gate, and I think it really adds a bit of style. We did attach some chicken wire on the lower section to be doubly sure that the dogs couldn't nip through.

The front garden
We have beds alongside the house in the front garden, as well as in front of the garden wall that screens us from the road. Bunny suggested putting in a parterre of box at the front of the house, but we decided it would be too much work. We put in little box hedges around some of the beds (before we were aware of problems with box blight and box tree caterpillars), and they look very attractive.

Fortunately, they've never had blight, but they certainly have been attacked by box tree caterpillars. We use all the potions possible to get rid of them, and so far, we've succeeded and they still look good. If I ever put in hedging like that again, though, I'd choose yew instead. I think yew is the best for hedging.

Kevin, our gardener, in the vegetable garden checking early-sown plants.

In the front garden, brick-edged beds filled with perennials and shrubs, backed by yew hedging, help to screen us from the road.

*Gardening, like cookery,
is a huge and fascinating
subject that I'm always eager
to learn more about*

Chapter 2
How I Garden

Gardening Over the Years

I have gardened for many years, and although I'm not trained and far from being a professional, I have learned quite a lot about what plants I like best, how to care for them, and what's needed in terms of design to make a garden look good.

As well as learning a lot from being a practical, hands-on gardener, I've gained a lot of knowledge from visiting great gardens and nurseries, sharing my interest with horticulturally minded friends, and gathering information from books and websites. Gardening, like cookery, is a huge and fascinating subject that I'm always eager to learn more about.

Cooking and gardening

I love and understand cooking. There's a science and logic to cooking and there's also a science and a logic to gardening. With cooking, I always say in the first instance, follow the recipe exactly. After that, you can wander off and do things a bit differently, and it's the same with gardening.

There's lots of tried and tested rules on how to do things, but once you've an understanding, then you can start experimenting. For instance, if a plant is supposed to be in a sunny position, in a dry corner, or in damp conditions, then it's worth getting the positioning right first. Later, you can experiment and learn from trial and error. There's so much information out there these days, what with books, television, YouTube, and many great websites, you can't really go wrong.

Moving house

I took some of my favourite plants from Watercroft to our new garden in Henley. As soon as the house was on the market, I dug up things in the autumn, divided them, and put them in pots. I also had a sizable area with my cuttings and plants that people had given me over the years. When my son Will died, people gave us all sorts of things, including the white Christmas rose (*Helleborus niger*), and it was important for me that I brought some to our new home. I also took primroses that originally came from my mother's garden. It's important not to do this at the last minute. Fortunately, many of us know in advance when we plan to sell our home.

Books, TV, and websites

I like to have garden books by my bed. One of my favourites is Alan Titchmarsh's book *The Gardener's Almanac*, which he kindly gave me. It's full of information and ideas, and honestly, it is absolutely brilliant. I also like the series of books on practical gardening by D.G. Hessayon, which have titles such as *The Lawn Expert* and *The Greenhouse Expert*. When I first started gardening, I used to look at these books for advice, and although nowadays we've got the internet, I find reading a book so comforting.

I was asked to be on BBC Radio 4's *Desert Island Discs* with Kirsty Young in 2012. She asked what book I would take, and I said the *RHS A–Z Encyclopedia of Garden Plants*, as I would be dreaming about what I'd be putting in my garden and I was absolutely sure that I would be rescued. Over the years, it's been a great source of information and is packed full of good advice.

I watch BBC *Gardeners' World* like a hawk, and I think some websites are really useful for learning about gardening or looking at plants to buy. For online suppliers, I particularly like Crocus and Sarah Raven. I also check the RHS website for plant information.

It's amazing what a breath of fresh air the RHS shows are, it's just a pleasure to go, and these days, you can buy plants at many of them.

Visiting shows, gardens, and nurseries

When Will died, I think I took comfort in the garden. That was on 21 January 1989, and at the end of January, Claire White, who lived in the next village to us and whom I didn't know really well, rang and said she'd just got tickets for the RHS Chelsea Flower Show in May. I remember thinking that I didn't want to go. Anyway, I said how very kind, I'd love to go. I found out what everybody wore and bought myself a new jacket. Claire said we must get there early, so we arrived at 8 o'clock in the morning.

I am so glad I went – it's amazing what a breath of fresh air these shows are, it's just a pleasure to go, and these days, you can buy plants at many of them. Since then, I've been to many of the RHS shows, and I particularly love Chelsea and the Malvern Spring Festival, which has a great atmosphere. There is plenty of space, and you can fill your boot with garden plants.

I also like to visit rare plant fairs, where you find the very best plants and growers on hand to give you advice. Again, it's a lovely day out. You just need to check the internet for what's on and where.

I have always enjoyed visiting other gardens and they are a great place to find inspiration. I tend to go on one garden tour a year, organized either by the Garden Museum or with James Bolton at Border Lines. I usually go with a gardening friend and it makes a great day out.

If you live near an RHS garden, it is such a joy for a day out. We're very lucky as RHS Garden Wisley in Surrey is not far away and I visit as often as I can. I recommend either going very early or a bit later in the day, and take a friend who appreciates gardens, as then you have time for conversation while looking at the plants. I usually make it a day out and have a bit of lunch there as well. And of course, the RHS gardens all have plant sales areas, so once you've been inspired by the garden, you can buy lots of the plants and talk to the staff, who are invariably knowledgeable and helpful. I recommend taking advantage of those.

I'm forever visiting plant nurseries. They are great places to find healthy specimens of interesting varieties and often the staff are very knowledgeable. We have a very good local nursery in Henley called Toad Hall and another called Smith's in Uxbridge. They are both very lovely and I enjoy visiting them to see what they have for sale. The plants are well looked after and the staff are very helpful. I think it's good to support local growers. I'm also fond of the small Danesfield Nursery, where everything is home grown, and Hillier Garden Centre is reliable too.

When visiting nurseries, my advice is to go early and before the weekend, when the stocks are high and there's usually more parking spaces. Preferably do not go on a bank holiday as they are often at their busiest then. Unless you've got access to a greenhouse, don't be tempted to buy annual plants too early as nothing should go out before the end of May.

Go with a list of things that you need or are looking for. I find I often go somewhere with the idea of buying, say, grass seed and come back with a load of plants and no grass seed at all. Also, before buying, make quite sure that the plants are in good health, and particularly with shrubs, check that they have a good shape.

The National Garden Scheme

The Heaths, the previous owners of Watercroft, used to open the garden for the National Garden Scheme (NGS), so we started doing it when we took on the property and continued to do so for 20 years. We'd open for one day and would have stands selling plants and other things such as honey.

At one point, we had 700 visitors, which was too much, so after that, we decided to open by appointment only, five or so times a year. Lucy Young, my wonderful PA and jack of all trades for 36 years, would be the one answering the phone and would give priority to gardening clubs and those really keen groups of gardeners. After 20 years of opening gardens, you get a trowel, and I'm delighted that I got mine.

It was a huge honour when George Plumptre, who was then the chief executive of the NGS, asked me to be president in 2016. Having opened our gardens for more than 20 years, I was passionate about the charity and hoped I could bring more attention and support. It

was a joy to work with George and the team for nine years, until I handed over the presidency to my dear friend Alan Titchmarsh, who will take it to new levels and give it the devotion it deserves.

The NGS is a marvellous organization that lists more than 3,300 privately owned gardens, which are open on selected days of the year in order to raise money for health, nursing, and gardening charities, including Marie Curie, Macmillan Cancer Support, Hospice UK, Maggie's, Horatio's Garden, Parkinson's UK, Carers Trust, and Perennial. Since it began in 1927, the NGS has raised over £74 million for its beneficiaries.

Details of all the NGS gardens that are open are listed in their publication, *The Garden Visitor's Handbook*, often referred to as *The Yellow Book*, as well as online. There are gardens of all sizes, the main criteria being that they must offer at least 45 minutes of interest. Often, you'll find great, reasonably priced plants for sale, lovely afternoon teas, and you get to meet other gardeners. It really is a perfect way of spending an afternoon with a friend.

For one fund-raising event, we held an auction where various people offered their time that people could bid on. I offered tea with Mary Berry and was amazed that two people paid £5,000 each to take part and we made £10,000.

At one of the charity events, I bought a day with Bunny Guinness to visit her garden in Northamptonshire and have lunch. I took along Penny Godfrey and Anne Eastick, two of my Henley gardening girlfriends, and it was wonderful as Bunny was so generous with her advice and gardening tips.

In 2018, I opened the Horatio's Garden at the National Spinal Injuries Centre at Stoke Mandeville Hospital in Buckinghamshire. It was designed by Joe Swift and really is excellent, with little individual half-moon-shaped gardens suitable for wheelchair access and seating for visitors and families, along with a café and a greenhouse that patients can access from the garden.

I was delighted to pass on my presidency of the
NGS to my dear friend Alan Titchmarsh.

People who are in spinal units tend to be in hospital for a very long time, so it's a lovely way of keeping their spirits up. There are numerous Horatio's Gardens open around the country now, and these therapeutic spaces created to help people after spinal injuries have all been designed by leading designers and are really special. You can visit them on their open days for the NGS.

Don't be nervous about opening your garden for the NGS. If you do and have a sizable space, or can encourage a group of local gardens to open, visitors love to buy things to take away. Items such as honey, plants, pottery, or artwork are popular as are teas, coffees, and cakes! A treasure hunt for the children can work well too. It's all about sharing.

I opened the Horatio's Garden at the National Spinal Injuries Centre at Stoke Mandeville Hospital, Buckinghamshire, in 2018.

Q & A
Alan Titchmarsh
CBE DL VMH

Generous with his expertise, knowledge, and ideas, gardener and broadcaster Alan is an inspiration to me. I feel like he is my mentor and I'm full of admiration. His advice on mulching is well worth following to keep plants moist and in good health, and sharp secateurs really do make all the difference.

What's the best way of improving garden soil?

Whenever you cultivate the earth, dig in lots of well-rotted garden compost or manure. It helps sandy soil retain moisture and will help to break up heavy clay, which also benefits from helpings of sharp grit. Mulch your beds and borders every spring with a 2-inch (5-centimetre) layer of garden compost or chipped bark to seal in moisture and help keep down weeds.

What are your favourite climbing roses for a sunny wall?

Rosa 'Alister Stella Gray' is a soft yellow fading to creamy white with a glorious scent. It's great for training up an old fruit tree. 'Albertine' is a salmon-pink rambler. It only has one season of flowering but it's an old favourite. 'Mary Delany' is pink and virtually thornless. It flowers right through summer after its initial flush of bloom.

What are your favourite climbing roses for a shady wall?

'Paul's Himalayan Musk' has masses of small, fully double, pale pink flowers. It's a rambler and it has a single flush in June, but it's so spectacular. It's another good one for training up through an old fruit tree. 'The Generous Gardener' is one of David Austin's best varieties.

It's repeat flowering with good foliage as well as pink flowers. 'Crimson Shower' is a rich red rambler. It's an old favourite but still worth growing.

What plants do you recommend for acid soil?

Pieris has flower clusters like lily of the valley and bright red, new shoots in spring. Camellias are great in tubs of ericaceous compost if you don't have acid soil, and rhododendrons in all shapes, sizes, and colours.

What plants do you recommend for alkaline soil?

Clipped yew (*Taxus*) topiary offers form and interest to the garden all year round. Clip it in late summer and it will stay sharp all the way through the winter. Pinks are great border edgers with deliciously fragrant flowers. Lavender is a wonderful edger. The varieties *Lavandula angustifolia* 'Hidcote' and 'Munstead' are the best as they are compact growing. Take cuttings to replace plants after four or five years.

What trees do you recommend for a small garden?

Amelanchier lamarckii (snowy mespilus) has wonderful, white blossom in spring followed by pinkish-tinged new growth, which turns green and then offers bright autumn colour at the end of the season. *Malus* x *floribunda* (Japanese crab apple) is a modest-sized tree with blossom that is dark pink in bud and white when it opens. Japanese maples (*Acer*) are good in large containers where space is limited, but shelter them from drying winds. Some are low growing, others taller, with finely cut leaves of green or purple.

What is your favourite gardening tool or piece of kit?

Sharp secateurs – they're indispensable!

My Gardening Tips

Over the years, as well as taking advice from friends and reading avidly, I have learned a lot through trial and error. Here I share some of my best gardening tips.

Soil

The sort of soil you have in your garden has a huge impact on what you can grow successfully. It's worth knowing that the RHS offers members a soil-analysis service where you can pay to have your soil checked, and it's far better than a kit. There are numerous ways you can improve your soil, including digging in organic matter such as well-rotted manure or homemade compost, but it's invaluable to know what you're starting off with and the best way to go about improving it.

You can't change the pH of your soil, but you can always improve it. Once, though, I made a terrible mistake when trying to do just that. I'd contacted a local farmer about buying some cattle manure and said I didn't want anything less than a year old because I wanted it well rotted and didn't want it to be full of seeds that would come up as weeds. He said he had some wonderful, aged manure. However, when it came, yes, it was old but there was lots of straw with it. I won't make that mistake again! Not only did it mean we had lots of weeds growing but also the dogs picked up the straw and took it all over the lawn, making quite a mess. I should have inspected it before I bought it. The ideal manure is really dark and crumbly like Christmas pudding.

When buying a new plant, it's important to check what sort of soil it needs. Very often, I read articles in magazines and newspapers about a plant such as *Eucryphia*, which is so beautiful but needs acidic soil, so there's no way it would grow in the garden here. Some lucky people have both acid and alkaline in different parts of the garden but sadly we don't.

Deadheading

I love deadheading and do it all the time as it's a great way of encouraging more flowers. It works with most plants, and roses, in particular, respond really well to deadheading. I always use sharp, clean secateurs and just snip off all of the spent flower heads and add them to the compost.

I deadhead all the time and I'm brutal. As well as promoting more flowers, taking off fading and dead flowers makes the plant look neater. Before we go away on holiday, say, in August, I take off every head that looks as if it's going to bloom while I'm away as I find it keeps the strength in the plant to put on flowers for when we're back. There is nobody here to enjoy them, and it's a lovely surprise when you come back a fortnight later to find fresh, new blooms. It works especially well with the 'Chandos Beauty' roses. I do it with my pelargoniums too. I take off every single head and give them a good feed and water, and they're lovely to come back to.

Deadheading means plants have the energy to make flowers instead of producing seed or fruit. With things like daffodils, the energy goes back into the bulb, meaning it will be stronger for the next season.

From roses and pansies to pretty much anything in the border you want to flower for longer, deadheading is essential.

For plants that self-seed prolifically, deadheading will mean you won't get new plants popping up all over. So it's worth bearing in mind if you do want some self-sown plants or you want to leave some seeds for the birds. And obviously, some seeds such as honesty look rather nice in the down season and the same goes for poppies. From roses and pansies to pretty much anything in the border you want to flower for longer, it does help.

Deadheading couldn't be easier. You use clean, sharp secateurs and cut off the flowerhead above the next flower bud, leaf, or side shoot.

With some plants, such as *Nepeta*, *Alchemilla mollis*, and hardy geraniums, once they have flowered in late July, you can cut the whole thing close to the ground and, with any luck and a good feed and watering, they will sprout back with fresh, new growth, which helps make the garden look rejuvenated and less tired.

A word of warning with *Plumbago*, a glorious, tender blue shrub. I gave my neighbour Anne Eastick, a dedicated gardener, some cuttings of the dark blue *Plumbago auriculata* that I had been given (I didn't trust myself to pot them up for her). She grew them into little rooted plants, and I now have a large terracotta pot of *Plumbago* that I cherish. But the buds look very similar to what's left of the flower when they have gone over, so I put my glasses on and am very careful what I snip off.

Pruning

I was taught to prune by Margaret Thorpe, who ran gardening courses in Burnham. She taught me all the basics and made us think through the reasons why we do it. Initially, I thought it was simply because you're supposed to, so to speak, as a way of keeping control and getting rid of dead, diseased, or damaged wood. Margaret explained that it's important to prune as a way to promote growth and keep plants healthy and productive, as well as to encourage a good shape and help to improve air circulation.

I've had that in my head ever since. It's easy to get overwhelmed with all the rules about pruning, but if you understand why you're doing it and how a plant grows, then it's not such a mystery.

One of the most important things I've learned with pruning is that it's important to know when and on which branches the next year's flowers will appear. For example, with my Japanese quince (*Chaenomeles japonica*), I prune annually just after it's finished flowering. It always flowers on growth made in the previous year, so by cutting after flowering, you can cut out the older wood and the plant has a good chance of putting on new growth and toughening

Sharp snips are essential to create a clean finish on topiary.

up before winter. It's the same with forsythia, lilac, *Philadelphus*, and viburnum. You must prune immediately after flowering. If you prune later or in winter, you may inadvertently cut off next year's flowering stems. Actually, it's Kevin, our gardener, who does most of the pruning.

I'm not a fan of letting weeds run wild in the garden. To my mind, you've got to get rid of the weeds, but often it takes time and continued effort.

We keep our secateurs, pruning saw, and loppers clean and sharp and wipe them when we move between plants so that we don't inadvertently spread disease. I know that some people occasionally spray with disinfectant too.

It's important to cut just above a bud and at an angle of around 45 degrees with the cut slanting away from the bud so that any water drains away from it. Ideally, choose an outward-facing bud so that plants don't end up growing inwards.

Some plants are tougher than others and respond really well to a hard prune. For example, we have a buddleia that grows for Britain, and we cut it right to the ground and it came back beautifully. I find my *Magnolia grandiflora* responds well to pruning too. Often, if a plant like that is a good age, it'll come back even if you cut it hard.

I no longer go up ladders and I would suggest that nobody my age goes up a ladder either. It's not worth the risk; far better to get someone younger to do it.

If my grandsons, Hobie and Louis, are over they will help out with a bit of pruning. I'll give them a pair of snips each and they will help shape our *Photinia* x *fraseri* 'Red Robin' shrubs. I stand and watch them, and they really love cutting things back.

Pruning raspberries
There are two approaches with raspberries, depending on whether you have summer- or autumn-fruiting varieties. Summer-fruiting

raspberries produce fruit on one-year-old canes. After they've fruited, I cut the canes right down to soil level. As the new canes develop for the following year, I just tie those into their supports, pruning out any that look a bit weak. I aim for about 6 inches (15 centimetres) between the new canes.

I find autumn-fruiting varieties of raspberries much easier to deal with. They fruit on the current season's canes, so I simply cut these all right down to the ground in winter. The new canes shoot up in spring, and as these tend to be shorter, they don't tend to need any staking.

Tackling weeds

I read that someone once wrote that a weed is just a plant in the wrong place, but I'm not a fan of letting weeds run wild and like to get rid of them, particularly perennial weeds. When we first moved into the Red House, we covered the borders with sheets of thick, black polythene for two years to get rid of the perennial weeds, bindweed, and ground elder. It's a long time to wait but it was worth it as it really did them in. Here in Henley, we battle with a patch of bindweed that comes under a wall from next door. We let it grow and then spray it. It helps, but it's a continual, ongoing battle.

Getting rid of ground elder is a real struggle if you have to dig it out, and anyway, I'm no good at digging. We've found that the best way is to completely block out any light with black polythene. After that, we plant the ground so densely that there isn't enough space for new weeds to take hold, and if any do manage to come up, then our last resort is to spray them.

In our last garden, we started to get weeds coming up through the alstroemeria, so after they'd finished flowering, I lifted them out of the picking bed, spread the roots out on a garden table, picked out all of the white roots of the bindweed, and then replanted them. It was a lot of work but it was a great success. To my mind, you've got to get rid of the weeds, but often it's a real fight and takes time and continued effort.

Planting advice

When I put a plant in the garden, I always dig a hole bigger than I need and often put in a bit of fish, blood, and bone with the soil. I pour in water to make a puddle, and once that has drained away, I position my plant, fill up the hole with the soil, then stamp all round it so that it's firmly in the ground. Then I give it a good water to settle in the roots.

I leave the plant to establish itself, and if the leaves go limp after about three or four weeks, I might give it some more water. This approach seems to work for me.

Micro-herbs

I had a go at growing micro-herbs, which are simply little seedlings of leafy herbs that you cut before they grow to full size. They were fun to grow and we used an old wine box, which looked quite smart.

We filled it with multipurpose compost and simply sowed the seeds densely but evenly. We put them in a spot with plenty of light and kept them well watered, and they germinated in no time at all – just days really. You harvest them by snipping off with scissors and they are great added to salads and garnishes. It's fun to do and cheap.

Supporting plants

Some perennials, especially those that are tall, with lush growth or heavy flowers, can collapse as they grow or are prone to toppling over in wind or heavy rain. Staking can help keep them upright and limit damage. That way, the new growth will grow through the support, helping to hide it and make everything look more natural.

Over the years, I have learned that with staking, it's always better to stake before you think you need it. Plants never look as good if you stake them too late on – they always look a bit trussed up and unnatural. If you have Michaelmas daisies (*Symphyotrichum novi-belgii*), for instance, and they grow to, say, 3 feet (1 metre) high,

I grow delphiniums through a frame to stop the large flower heads falling over.

then put in supports when they reach a foot (30 centimetres) high. You can use all sorts of things to stake plants, such as twiggy branches, bamboo canes with string, smart metal supports, or even pig wire held on a discreet frame for plants to grow through. Kevin is a past master at staking with canes and deftly tying up with twine.

Protecting plants

At our previous garden at Watercroft, we had four standard bay trees, and in the first winters, all of them got frosted. From then on for the first three years, we put a double layer of black netting over the top and tied loosely beneath. You hardly noticed it and it did the job of protecting them. I've done the same in Henley with the bay trees here that we have on the terrace.

Lawn care

We started the lawn from seed and water it and feed it well. We have metal edging that looks rather smart and makes the edges easier to maintain. Kevin mows the lawn every week, reseeds areas that need it, and rakes it over to get rid of any moss. We like having it mowed regularly because it's nice having the traditional stripes, and I love playing croquet.

Houseplants

I've found one of the most important things with houseplants is to work out what each plant needs and get the watering regime right. I've got a lovely white Christmas cactus that I'm very excited about. I'm afraid that I overwatered it and it really wasn't at all happy. I had it drying out all summer just with a dash of water and it's just starting to flower again.

One of the most important things with houseplants is to work out what each plant needs and get the watering regime right.

I feed my houseplants often, but it's such a temptation to overuse plant feed, although, invariably, it does tell you on the side of the bottle what the dosage should be.

Another good trick with houseplants is to regularly turn the pot around so that plants grow straighter rather than always leaning towards the light. It's often better not to have direct sunlight as it can scorch the leaves. Orchids like the bright, indirect sunlight on east- or west-facing windows. The temperature in the house is very important – hot in the day followed by cold at night is not ideal.

Planning a new garden

I've learned what matters most when planning a new garden and it's best to start by considering the soil – find out what you've got and improve where necessary. Try to choose the right plant for the right place, checking which way the garden faces. Plant sun-loving plants facing south, and use plants that tolerate shade in more shady areas. I always aim for colour and interest all year round and plan that into my planting. Choose plants of the right height for the borders, low at the front and gradually gaining height towards the back. When it comes to edible crops, I only grow what I like to eat! Lastly, never rush things. Gardening takes time and patience.

Edging plants

I like having low-growing plants at the front of the borders and especially if they gently spill over the low retaining wall, as it softens the line of the bricks. These are five of my favourites:
- aubretias
- dwarf sedums
- *Nepeta racemosa* 'Walker's Low' (catmint)
- *Stachys byzantina* 'Silver Carpet' (lamb's ear)
- veronicas

Flowers and foliage for cutting

My mother always liked to have freshly cut flowers from the garden in the house, and I'm exactly the same. One thing that I learned

I enjoy picking lily of the valley for the house as the scent is exceptionally good.

from my mother is that when you have two lots of flower displays in one room, then it's best if they can relate to one another somehow. For instance, they can be flowers that match or have some sort of visual connection. It may be that you use a bigger vase of the same flowers as a centrepiece to the room and then have a smaller vase at the table.

I pick flowers early in the morning or late at night and put them in water in a cool place before arranging them. It's important to cut a little bit off the bottom of the stem before you put them in the vase, as freshly cut stems can take up the water more readily. Here are some of my favourites.

Shrubs
- *Camellia japonica* (camellia)
- *Chaenomeles japonica* (Japanese quince)
- *Eucalyptus gunnii* (cider gum)
- forsythia, choose a shade that you like best
- hydrangeas, white varieties

Bulbs and corms
- *Cyclamen hederifolium* and *C. coum* (ivy-leaved and eastern cyclamen)
- daffodils: *Narcissus* 'Rijnveld's Early Sensation', 'Bridal Crown', 'Silver Chimes', 'February Gold', 'Hawera', 'Tête-à-tête', and 'Toto'
- dahlias: *Dahlia* 'Rip City', 'Silver Years', and *D. merckii*
- gladioli, the pink and white cultivars
- *Iris unguicularis* and *I. unguicularis* 'Mary Barnard' (Algerian iris)
- lilies, the pink and white cultivars
- snowdrops: *Galanthus elwesii* and *G. elwesii* 'Grumpy'
- tulips: *Tulipa* 'Angélique', 'Spring Green', and 'China Town'

Perennials and annuals
- *Aconitum* (monk's hood) – take care with this as it is poisonous
- *Alchemilla mollis* (lady's mantle)

Camellia japonica
(camellia)

Iris unguicularis *'Mary Barnard'*
(Algerian iris)

Antirrhinum tortuosum
(snapdragon)

Helleborus niger
(Christmas rose)

I've always loved estate railing as it's perfect for keeping the dogs safely in the back garden when the front gate is open. When they were puppies, I added chicken wire to stop them getting through it.

- *Alstroemeria* Summer Paradise Series (Peruvian lily)
- *Antirrhinum tortuosum* (snapdragon), whites and pinks
- *Aster* x *frikartii* 'Mönch' (aster)
- *Cosmos bipinnatus* Sonata Series (cosmea)
- *Dianthus barbatus* (sweet william)
- *Echinacea*, especially the wine-red ones with petals that don't droop, such as 'SunSeekers Red' and 'SunSeekers Pomegranate'
- *Helleborus niger* (Christmas rose)
- *Lathyrus* (sweet peas) in pinks, whites, and blues
- *Pelargonium* 'Sweet Mimosa' (geranium)
- *Phlox paniculata* 'White Admiral' (perennial phlox)
- *Primula vulgaris* (primrose)
- *Rosa* 'Chandos Beauty'
- *Salvia* 'Amistad', *S. farinacea* 'Victoria Blue', and *S. nemorosa* 'Caradonna' (sage, Balkan clary)
- sedums, particularly the taller varieties
- zinnias, a mix of different colours is best

Climbers

I love things running along walls, although unfortunately, here in Henley we don't really have much wall to work with. Some of my favourites include:

- *Clematis* 'Hagley Hybrid'
- climbing roses, such as *Rosa* 'Paul's Himalayan Musk', 'Rambling Rector', and 'Graham Thomas'
- *Magnolia grandiflora* 'Exmouth' (evergreen magnolia), which is technically not a climber but can be trained against a wall to give the appearance of a climber
- *Trachelospermum jasminoides* (star jasmine), which has lovely, sweetly scented, white flowers in spring or summer

Evergreen hedging and topiary

Evergreen hedging and clipped forms provide year-round structure and interest in the garden and make a great backdrop to other plantings. Yew is my favourite.

Box (*Buxus*)
My son Thomas has been married for some 20 or so years now, and we bought the box topiary spirals for his wedding day to go at the entrance of the marquee. Originally, they were in much smaller pots and were fine, until all of a sudden, they started to look dreadful. I had a rummage around inside and saw that, in fact, the wire that had been put in to train them into the spiral shape had begun strangling the stem. I cut the wire away and they continued looking dreadful for a few years, but gradually they recovered and started filling out. Fortunately, these spirals have never had box blight, and in my experience, the single specimens, unlike hedging, don't seem to suffer from it as much.

I do check obsessively for box tree caterpillar – it's a bit like looking for nits in children's hair – and as soon as I see any sign of it, we spray them immediately. Given the current problems with box blight and box tree caterpillar, I wouldn't plant box again as it's too much of a struggle to keep it looking healthy these days, and if you do a bit of research, you'll find there are a whole load of alternatives, such as yew (*Taxus*) and small-leaved holly (*Ilex crenata*), that you can use instead of box.

We grow our topiary spirals in containers, so we keep them well watered and clip them regularly – usually around June and again in August or September – to keep their shape looking nice and crisp. We find they also benefit from a sprinkling of slow-release fertilizer in spring.

Yew (*Taxus*)
We put in the yew hedging a year after we moved to Henley, and it's grown really well. I think this is largely because we put in a leaky hose to make sure it was watered regularly while it got established. We had the hose on a timer as it's more economical to water in the middle of the night and the water doesn't evaporate as quickly. We don't water the yew now, unless we're experiencing extremely dry weather and you see the edges are getting brown, in which case, we'll put the hose back on.

At either end of the main lawn, we have put in yew hedging that we are pruning to create shoulders, inspired by those at the Laskett, Sir Roy Strong's garden in Herefordshire.

My Gardening Tips

We're trying to develop the hedging at either end of the lawn so that they have a sloping side, a sort of shoulder. I'm copying those I admired at the Laskett, Sir Roy Strong's garden in Herefordshire. We had them like that at our previous house, and Kevin knows how to do it. The sloping shoulders are coming along beautifully.

Being evergreen and dense, yew makes a great hedge and unlike box, it doesn't suffer from blight or get attacked by box tree caterpillar. We now only have mainly yew, with just a little bit of box because when we put box in six years ago, there wasn't the caterpillar, which causes such terrible damage.

Yew has a reputation for being slow growing, but in fact, in good soil and with adequate watering, it can put on around 12 inches (30 centimetres) of growth each year. They like to grow in moist, well-drained soil and are fine in both full sun and full shade.

Before we plant, we always dig over the soil and add in well-rotted manure or garden compost to give them a good start. For hedging, we put plants in around 2 feet (60 centimetres) apart. Although we've found they definitely benefit from being well watered while getting established, in the long term, they don't like to have their roots overly wet as they can suffer from rot.

While they are getting established, we avoid cutting off the growing tips as this can stall their growth. Now our hedges are more established, we trim them once a year anytime from September to October. It's a big job but it's worth it. Yew is one of the most forgiving of hedges as it can make new shoots even on old wood, so we don't have to worry if we make a mistake as it can grow again. I'm very fortunate as Kevin gardens for us every Thursday all year round, and he keeps back a lot of the pruning jobs to do in the down season.

Gardening tools and equipment

My favourite tool is my faithful swoe, a type of hoe with three sharp edges. It's absolutely excellent. When I did the Aga cooking school

I love using a swoe, my favourite tool, to weed between plants.

at Watercroft, we used to go out and hoe in the evening. We had a big vegetable garden and my friend Penny Tetley and I would have a glass of something – a gin and tonic or some wine – and we'd each have a swoe and chat away while gardening. It was a lovely way to spend an evening before supper. There would always be lots of good things left over after the Aga course, so we didn't have to worry about cooking.

Old gardening tools are often the best, and you can buy second-hand ones in antique shops or junk shops, or you can pick them up in house clearances. I would much rather have those than buying brand-new ones. We've used pretty much the same tools for more than 50 years. I still have the little spade we were given as one of our wedding presents. It came from Richard Patterson, who had an ironmonger's business and was a very great friend. I also like a long-handled trowel and steer away from anything plastic.

I recommend having a pair of good secateurs. The ones from Felco are excellent, and they offer a service to resharpen them for you. Actually, I buy their less expensive ones because they're lighter for my hands.

When I'm gardening, I force myself to put gloves on to protect my hands, and I like the ones that fit fairly tightly and have some form of waterproofing. I avoid the ones that are gimmicky in different colours or with flowers on them.

I prefer the very, very lightweight wheelbarrows. I have the sort with tyres that don't need redoing and one long handle Smart Cart. I ordered it in a rash moment at Chelsea and it cost a lot of money, but I've now had it for about 20 years so it was money well spent.

I also like the slate labels and use a permanent white Edding paint marker pen to write on them as it lasts really well.

We have a watering system in the garden, which makes things easier as one gets older. I have devices for spraying as I do spray the roses and the box plants for pests and diseases, as I feel needs must, but wouldn't dream of spraying anything in the vegetable garden.

We store all the tools along with plant supports in our shed. It's reasonably tidy and I love it. We have a cupboard in there where we have lots of different things tucked away just in case, spares, things we don't really need, and things we've forgotten about.

My mistakes

I've learned that when you go to buy a specific plant, perhaps you even go to a specific nursery, if the plant isn't quite right or isn't just what you want, or perhaps it's misshapen or not healthy, then it's best to draw breath, go home, and buy it somewhere else.

Just this year, I went too early to buy cucumber plants. And there they were, looking absolutely lovely at the beginning of May, and I put one in the greenhouse and looked after it. But shortly afterwards, the bottom of the plant just seemed to break off. Since coming to Henley, I've found a gardening kindred spirit in Penny Godfrey. We both bought cucumber plants too early, which wilted, and we ended up having to buy more. My advice is: don't be tempted to buy things too early but wait until it's warmer.

I made a big mistake by planting a beetroot variety called 'Chioggia', which has beautiful white rings when cut. I was given some seeds, so I put in two rows of them, and they got going really early. Eventually, I harvested them and they looked spectacular, but when you cook them, they turn white and aren't anywhere near as pretty. Next time, I will put in only 10 or so plants, harvest them early, and slice very thinly with a mandolin to eat raw. I learned my lesson.

As a family, we love eating outside, and I bought a sun parasol that goes into the centre of the table. However, it's far too big and difficult to open out without having to ask for help, and I realized it's better to have a big, free-standing umbrella with an arm that hovers over the table. It's so much better than the sort that you have to put in the middle of the table, as with those, you can't move them and get shade where you want it. You can even get free-standing ones with wheels so they are easy to move.

I ask myself if it's a mistake to keep having hollyhocks. My husband loves them so I still grow them, but they suffer from rust and anything near them takes it on too.

Q & A
Polly Nicholson

The queen of tulips and holder of the National Collection of Tulipa (historic), Polly knows everything about this beautiful flower. It's a delight to visit her garden, which is occasionally open for the NGS. She is the delightful daughter of close friends Hylton and Charlotte Bayntun-Coward, who were great friends in Bath. Sadly, they are no longer with us. Over the years, I've watched Polly flourish.

What are your favourite early and late varieties of tulips?

My favourite early tulips are the species varieties (division 15) that I have established in the herbaceous borders running through our series of walled gardens. *Tulipa* 'Peppermintstick' is pink-and-white candy striped, opening wide to the sun during the daytime and closing to a neat point come evening, when the light levels reduce. Another favourite is *T. orphanidea* Whittallii Group (commonly sold as *T. whittallii*), which starts khaki before opening to bronze, and holds on to its petals for weeks on end as they dry and desiccate while still in situ. *T. sylvestris*, known as the wild tulip, romps through our woodland beds at the foot of the garden, its yellow reflexed petals adding colour and movement at an otherwise dreary time of year.

At the other end of the season, I favour double lates massed together in large containers, choosing a range of cultivars in either complementary or clashing colour schemes. Their heavy heads and deeply ruffled petals are reminiscent of peonies – indeed, they are known as peony flowered.

Do you have any particular advice on planting tulips in the ground and in containers?

Above all else, tulips want good drainage, so I plant my special historic tulips on a layer of horticultural sand in November and December each year, lifting them the following summer after they have flowered and (hopefully) dried out. The sand prevents them from rotting during wet periods and helps preserve the health of the collection.

In containers, I forgo the sand, simply ensuring I have a free-draining mix with crocks at the bottom. I plant the bulbs close together but not touching, in a single layer, and tend not to combine them with other flowers.

Which tulips are the most reliably perennial and come back each year?

Species tulips are the most reliable, as they are the original, wild tulips and their hybrids. Once established, they form ever-increasing colonies that can be left in the ground all year round.

Of the annual or garden tulips, the Viridiflora (division 8) tulips are the best at coming back. I like to think that the green in their petals gives photosynthesis an extra boost.

Which tulips do you recommend picking for the house?

Tulips for cutting are my guilty pleasure, as I experiment with hundreds of varieties each year in the knowledge that they are one-season wonders. We harvest them with the bulb attached for extra stem length. This means the bulbs will not grow properly again as the stem and leaves have been removed, but they do go into the compost heap.

Parrot tulips such as 'Black Parrot', 'Flaming Parrot', or 'Apricot Parrot' are perfect for picking, and I am passionate about the so-called French tulips, 'Dordogne', 'Françoise', and 'Menton', which make amazing displays with their super-long, strong stems reaching almost a metre (3 feet).

What is your favourite gardening tool or piece of kit?

I am a believer in chicken wire 'hats' to keep squirrels from eating container displays. We mould chicken wire into a conical shape to fit each container. When the foliage has reached about 8 to 10 centimetres (3 to 4 inches) tall and the bulbs are well rooted, we remove the 'hats'.

Sometimes, the squirrels will launch an opportunistic attack after the wire is removed – in such cases, we will scatter chilli flakes between the tulips.

There is always something to enjoy in the garden, whatever the season, from the first spring bulbs to bringing in my Christmas trees

Chapter 3

My Gardening Year

Spring

For me, spring is the most exciting part of the year, as it's full of promise and there's something about early flowering plants that really lifts the spirits. I love it when I'm driving in the countryside and spot the first sprigs of hawthorn coming to show green. It really is just the best time as you've all the anticipation of waiting for things to happen, and even though there's not a huge amount going on, I like that everything is pruned back and ready to go.

Spring displays

In the garden, we've planted lots of the daffodil 'Rijnveld's Early Sensation', which, as the name suggests, flowers in very early spring. I first spotted it in a garden I visited in Salcombe in Devon, where it was flowering in January, most likely because it's further south and a bit warmer there compared to where we are. At our previous house, Watercroft, I planted it all along the outside wall on the roadside. Here, at our garden in Henley, I've planted it where you can see it as you walk through the front gate. And I love looking out for it as I come up the drive when I arrive home. I've planted a number of other daffodils around other parts of the garden too, including the early 'Tête-à-tête' and 'February Gold'.

I like using daffodils as a cut flower around the house, particularly the scented ones. I always pick them while they are still in bud, as it's such a pleasure to watch them coming into flower. I've read that it's best not to mix daffodils in a vase with other things, but to be honest, I have never taken too much notice of that. I particularly like combining them with some stems of winter-flowering honeysuckle (*Lonicera fragrantissima*), and if I've been on a walk and find some catkins, then I like to add those in too. I also like using the stems of forsythia and cornelian cherry (*Cornus mas*), both of which have pretty yellow flowers early in the year.

I used to love putting out displays of the scented daffodils called paper white when I had visitors, as the smell really is wonderful, but they didn't always bloom when I needed them most, such as for guests coming over, and I found it so sad that they don't reflower when you plant them outdoors afterwards. They work out jolly expensive for something that you end up chucking away, so I've decided enough is enough and I'm not growing them any more. That said, I do sometimes buy them as cut flowers.

Following on from daffodils, I have early and late tulips. At the front of the house, under the white hydrangea 'Annabelle', I've planted one of my favourite tulips, which is called 'Angélique'. In late autumn, usually around October but definitely before Christmas, we cut the hydrangea down to the ground so that the tulips appear through the bare soil before the shoots of the hydrangea begin to emerge. Underplanting like this can work really well as long as you get the timing right.

I like using daffodils as a cut flower around the house, particularly the scented ones. I always pick them while they are still in bud.

Although tulips are perennial, they don't always come back as strong after the first year. Sarah Raven advised me to plant my tulips deep, so that's exactly what I do, and I'm convinced that this helps them come back. Anyway, I always buy more bulbs to add in to keep the displays looking good from year to year.

I have a thing about a white wallflower I have – I'm not sure of its Latin name, but it could be *Erysimum cheiri* 'Ivory White' or 'Rysi Moon'. I think it looks lovely growing among the blue hyacinths. Ideally, I plant these in a place where I can see them daily, either somewhere that I walk past regularly or where I can enjoy them from inside the house, because while it's still cold outdoors, I don't always feel like going into the garden. Alternatively, you can plant them in a place where you grow them specifically for picking.

I always think of spring as blue, white, and yellow, but I prefer to see just the blue and the white together with crocus. They have

The blossom on this horse chestnut tree is spectacular in late spring. Sadly, in late summer, the leaves turn brown due to leaf miner, but each year when spring comes, the tree recovers.

them like that at the RHS Garden Wisley too, although I had mine in those colours before I saw their amazing displays, so I'm not copying.

That said, I am inspired by Wisley all the time. Gardening is all about learning, and when I visit other gardens and places such as Kew and Wisley, I'll often look at plants and think, don't they look lush and beautiful, but when you get them home from the nursery or garden centre, you've really got to find the best place for them and look after their needs.

I try to order my spring bulbs so that they are delivered in September. You can find lots of inspiration in bulb catalogues, many of which are really good and give details of the flowering times, and if you plant accordingly, you can have wonderful displays from the beginning until the end of spring.

We have an entrance gate that everyone has to walk through to get to the house, and I try to put things there that are of interest. For instance, we've got some little mounds of sedums as well as *Veronica* that are just emerging and will spill nicely over the brick wall.

I love picking lily of the valley to display in a small vase in the house.

Q & A
Sarah Raven

Sarah is an expert gardener, cook, and writer, and she taught me all I know about growing cut flowers, container planting, and being brave with colours. Her plant choice is always exceptional and she gives such fantastic advice, although I'm not sure I'll be using a hori hori knife as it sounds too dangerous for me!

What are your top 10 flowers or plants for cutting for the house?

Flowers
Cosmos **'Purity'** has pure white, generous saucer flowers with lovely, bright green, ferny foliage.
Cosmos **'Rubenza'** is a rich, carmine-crimson cut-and-come-again annual that flowers all summer long.
Dahlia **'Labyrinth'** is a beautiful, soft apricot dahlia fading to white with curvy petals.
Dahlia **'Sissinghurst'** is one of the most beautiful dahlias you'll ever find, with deep crimson, velvet petals and a creamy coffee-coloured petal edge. It has a vase life of more than a week.
Pelargonium **'Attar of Roses'** lasts a month in the vase, with delicious, fragrant leaves and pretty flowers, ideal as mini sprigs to scatter in bedrooms and bathrooms.
Rosa **'Duchess of Cornwall'** opens coral and fades to soft pink with a great scent and vase life, and it's super healthy and long-flowering.
Tulipa **'White Valley'** lasts seven to 10 days in water and you need just a few of its lovely, peony-like, white flowers to fill a vase.

Foliage
Ammi majus (bishop's flower) is a white flower, rather like cow parsley, that is the perfect filler for June or July vases,

and, if autumn sown, gets to 2.5 metres (8 feet) tall!

Cerinthe is one of my favourites for vases, either as foliage or on its own. Sear the stem ends in boiling water for 10 seconds before arranging them.

Euphorbia oblongata (Balkan spurge) has flat, plateau-forming, acid-green flowers that last 10 days in a vase and make the best scaffolding for almost any bunch of flowers. Take care not to get sap on your skin or in your eyes.

How do you make a bulb lasagne?

This is where you layer bulbs one on top of another in storeys like a lasagne, with compost forming the padding in between. Tulips tend to go in deepest, with the more delicate narcissus in the next layer up, and then maybe a miniature iris or crocus to flower first in February and March.

Do you have any tips for growing sweet peas?

Sweet peas are super-hungry and thirsty plants that really benefit from lots of farmyard manure added to their planting position, and then plenty of water to soak their roots if we have a dry spell. They also need a robust teepee, ideally standing 2.2 metres (7 feet) tall, that they can climb over.

Have you come across any new plants that you are particularly excited about?

I always am! I am so excited about lots of new dahlias we are breeding and cultivating to launch in the next couple of years. *Dahlia* 'Sissinghurst' turns out to have an exceptionally long vase life, and I adore our new dahlia 'Tom's Choice', which is elegant, glamorous, and busy with pollinators whenever the sun shines. In the winter and early spring, I'm also very keen on lots of new pansies and violas such as *Viola cornuta* 'HoneyFrost' and 'Brush Strokes', which last over a week in a vase if you sear the stem ends. And the highly scented, early-flowering *Narcissus* 'Polar Hunter' is an exceptional newbie too.

What is your favourite gardening tool or piece of kit?

We are all obsessed with the hori hori, a Japanese tool and halfway between a trowel and a knife. It's fantastic for planting and makes light work of it even in our heavy clay soil. And I love my florist's snips with orange handles. They're cheap and cheerful but work perfectly, with sharp blades that can be sharpened as and when I need to. I never have either of these far from my gardening coat pocket.

Key spring plants

Some of my earliest memories of plants are those that relate to spring, and I always look forward to seeing the first buds coming into flower and leaves unfurling. On the following pages are some of my favourites for March through to May.

Bougainvillea

I've grown a bougainvillea for years in a large pot and it flowers well. I keep it well fed and watered. In winter, all the leaves drop off and it looks dead. I always carefully cover it with horticultural fleece and give it the minimum amount of water. In spring, I water it again, then put it outside at the end of May and miraculously it comes back!

Chaenomeles japonica (Japanese quince)

I love Japanese quince, and definitely recommend growing it as it is great for picking. We grew it in our garden at the Red House, and here we've got a nice pinky-red one along a wall. You can find them in a number of different colours from white and peach to scarlet. They flower in early spring, just before the daffodils and other spring bulbs come out. It's often a time when there's not much else out, so their pretty flowers are always particularly welcome.

They grow to about 3 feet (1 metre) tall. I like to put big branches of it in a vase I have that is quite elegant with a narrow top and a handle on one side. They look really modern and last so well in the vase, unlike, say, cherry blossom, which is over the day after you pick it. This lasts for ages and really is lovely.

It's an easy-going shrub to grow that is tolerant of a wide range of conditions, and it can be left to grow as a free-standing specimen or trained up a wall or fence. It makes flowers on the previous year's growth, so we prune it directly after it has finished flowering.

This bougainvillea enjoys my sunny patio and flowers through to the end of summer.

Chaenomeles japonica
(Japanese quince)

Citrus x limon *(lemon)*

Convallaria majalis
(lily of the valley)

Crocus

Spring

***Citrus* x *limon* (lemon)**
We have a lemon tree in a large terracotta pot, and it's my absolute pride and joy. Citrus trees are not generally hardy in the UK, so we always bring our lemon tree into the greenhouse well before the frost and leave it there over winter, well wrapped up in horticultural fleece. When all danger of frost has gone, we carry it back outdoors again to a nice sunny, sheltered spot where we can enjoy it.

The leaves are lovely and glossy, and in spring, it produces pretty, citrus-scented, white flowers that are followed by fruit. Although we water it regularly, citrus doesn't like becoming waterlogged, so we added crocks and plenty of grit to the pot when we planted it.

A good haircut in spring can make all the difference. They are quite vigorous growers so they respond well. We recently pruned ours quite hard, and it came back beautifully. You have to encourage growth towards the middle, or it can start looking a bit empty. In summer, we feed it with a special citrus feed and take off all the fruit at the end of the season so that the tree can conserve its energy.

***Convallaria majalis* (lily of the valley)**
If you've got a shady area in the garden, then lily of the valley is worth the effort of growing. It's a hardy perennial and produces lush, green foliage and arching stems of sweetly scented, tiny, delicate, bell-shaped flowers in pure white in spring. It's low growing – 10 inches (25 centimetres) tall – so makes good ground cover.

As well as shade, lily of the valley likes moist, humus-rich soil, and if the conditions are right, it will happily spread around to make a dense carpet. When clumps become congested, then it's just a matter of dividing plants in autumn. My inspirational gardening friend Matt Pottage gave me a huge box of them in the green (with leaves), and we planted them in one of the shady borders. So far they are doing well and I've kept them well watered to get them established.

They look good in a vase, although it's worth finding a suitable shape and size to show them off. I like to pick around 20 heads and add in a few leaves. I'm going to try 'Vic Pawlowski's Gold' as recommended by Matt Pottage for its variegated foliage.

I like the idea of being inside the house and being able to see the first spring flowers appear in the garden.

Crocus

With crocus, I like to have simply the blue and white ones together and avoid growing yellow in the mix. If you want to see a really great example, it's worth going to RHS Garden Wisley where they also have just the blue and white crocus together in one huge drift. They are absolutely gorgeous.

We always plant our crocus in autumn, putting in the little bulbs to a depth of three times their size. They like a sunny spot in moist but well-drained soil best of all. After we've planted them in the ground, we always put some old netting over the top and peg it down, as it helps prevent the squirrels from digging them all up before they establish. I really like the idea of being inside the house and being able to see some of the first flowers appear in spring.

It's lovely to grow crocus as a dense carpet rather than having single ones at a distance from one another, and I think they work particularly well around the base of a deciduous tree. I've found that it's best not to put them around evergreens as they really need to have a decent amount of light in order to thrive.

I rather like 'Jeanne d'Arc', which has large, pure white, goblet-shaped flowers, stained purple at the base and bright orange stamens. We are also trying to naturalize the early crocus (*Crocus tommasinianus*) in the lawn. It has small, lilac to deep violet flowers in early spring that sometimes are slightly paler on the outsides of the petals. They do best in well-drained soil in full sun. One they grow at Wisley that I like is 'Pickwick', and these are very pretty with large, silvery-grey flowers striped the length of the petals with veins of dark purple and gold-orange stamens.

Erysimum cheiri (wallflower)

I'm afraid I don't have the proper names for these white wallflowers that I'm so fond of, but they are most likely *Erysimum cheiri* 'Ivory

White'. I bought some of these beautiful plants from our local nursery, Smiths in Uxbridge. I'd never seen them before and thought they could look good in the garden as well as in pots with some spring-flowering bulbs. They were absolutely lovely, lasting several weeks, and I thought I'd have a go at trying to grow them myself from seed.

Once the plants had set seed, I pulled them up and laid them down in the greenhouse to dry with a tray beneath lined with brown paper. I left them until they dried out then shook them gently until the seeds came off. I stored the seed over winter then sowed them in the greenhouse in spring, and they've grown really well.

I'm so thrilled, although I noticed that a mouse had nibbled some leaves, so I've had to raise them up on top of some flowerpots, so they are not so easy to reach! I reckon I've caught them just in time. I've also bought some plug plants from Sarah Raven of another white variety called 'White Dame', which has a slightly different leaf. They have been very successful.

Most wallflowers are biennial, so if we are growing them from seed, we start them off in the greenhouse in spring, plant them out in autumn, and then have to wait for them to flower the following spring. You can also buy them as bare-root plants that you plant in autumn for displays the following year. They do best in moist, well-drained soil in a sunny or partially shaded spot.

Eucalyptus gunnii (cider gum)

I grow various sorts of eucalyptus tucked away out of sight at the back of the tennis court. The fresh leaves are so useful for cutting in spring when you haven't got enough flowers for a vase. Their slightly waxy, blue-grey leaves are evergreen so there's nearly always something I can pick.

Eucalyptus is renowned for growing quickly and some can reach up to 80 feet (25 metres) tall, but this species responds well to being hard pruned, so we take the top growth off to get bushy growth at the bottom. The added advantage of doing this is that the leaves remain small and rounded rather than becoming elongated as they do if left to their own devices, and these are useful to fill out flower arrangements in a jug. Ours look more like shrubs than trees. We prune in late winter to early spring before they start putting on growth.

Eucalyptus is native to Australia, so they are remarkably drought tolerant. In south England, they are generally hardy apart from very cold winters, so are best grown in a sheltered, sunny spot.

Exochorda x *macrantha* 'The Bride' (pearlbush)
'The Bride' is absolutely wonderful. We grew it at both the previous houses. It's a deciduous shrub with arching stems up to 6½ feet (2 metres) long that, from around April to May, bear lots of really pretty, pure white flowers. There's not so much flowering at that time of year, so it adds some much-needed interest.

After flowering is over, mid-green leaves emerge along the stems and, come autumn, these turn yellow and orange. We bought ours already fan-trained and planted it against a wall, attaching the stems to wires attached to the wall to hold it in place.

Exochorda likes full sun and well-drained, moist soil. In order to encourage flowering, we always prune it right after flowering has finished, cutting each flowering stem to about half. If you're buying *Exochorda* as a free-standing shrub, I would recommend the variety *E.* x *macrantha* 'Lotus Moon'. Make sure it has a good shape and is nice and compact and not straggly.

Ferns
I'm addicted to ferns and I always longed to have lots of them in the garden, so when we moved here, it was just a matter of finding the best place to put them. We've got this huge, evergreen oak to the right of the driveway, which is hundreds of years old and you can't even stretch your arms around it. It really is magnificent, although it drips a sugary syrup, I think from aphids, on top of cars and it drops leaves everywhere. Apart from that, it's lovely and it seemed the ideal place. I often think shade is a bonus; it's just a matter of understanding what you can grow there. I love watching the ferns as they unfurl in spring.

Erysimum cheiri
(wallflower)

Eucalyptus gunnii
(cider gum)

Exochorda x macrantha
'The Bride' (pearlbush)

I only ever want large-leaved, evergreen ferns because they provide interest throughout the year, so I went to various nurseries to see first-hand the ones I like best. I don't have any particular favourites (I'm not very good at Latin names), so I simply find those that I particularly like the look of, check they are healthy with strong, new growth, and buy those. Most of mine I found at Smiths at Uxbridge, where you see them growing prolifically.

I'm addicted to ferns and love watching the new leaves as they unfurl in spring.

When we first planted them beneath the tree, nothing much happened. I used to water them occasionally with a watering can, but then, because the soil was so dry, we decided to install a watering system that is activated to come on for 30 minutes at night. It was only then that the plants really took off. If you have evergreen ferns in a totally dry environment such as mine, then I recommend giving them a lot of water for the first two years to help them get their roots down. In my experience, they will come to nothing unless you take watering seriously.

Between the ferns, to fill out any gaps at the front, I planted some sweet woodruff (*Galium odoratum*) given to me by a friend, as well as some little *Cyclamen coum* and snowdrops. These little plants add more interest, particularly in spring, and seem good at fighting for their own space. I'm pleased to say that finally the fernery is really looking good.

There are so many different ferns out there and getting the right ones is quite fun. You know, people say, 'What can I give you for the garden, I want to bring something?', and I say, an evergreen fern, and I don't mind what they bring and I've got quite a lot now.

Evergreen ferns are supposed to go through the winter, but they do start looking a bit tatty, so at the beginning of summer, I take

I love ferns and prefer the evergreen ones, to give interest all year.

Spring

out all the dead leaves. I don't feel as if I've succeeded yet but am determined I will, as the ferns are a good way to bring interest, rather than have just bare ground.

Hippeastrum 'Apple Blossom' (amaryllis)

Amaryllis, or hippeastrum as they are also known, are so good, and its flamboyant, trumpet-shaped flowers are a welcome sight in early spring. There are quite a few colours to choose from, but this is my favourite. It has large, showy white flowers that have streaks of pink running through them and a pale green base beneath the stamens. These bulbs are tender so must be grown in pots indoors.

If I order online, I go for a reputable supplier, such as Parker's Wholesale (buying with a group of friends), as I want to get the biggest, strongest-looking bulbs possible. To plant them, I fill a pot with compost and simply sit three bulbs on top so that they are a bit above the rim of the pot.

Then I add a little more compost, firm it down gently, sprinkle on a top dressing of more grit, and then give it a good watering. They like a rich growing medium that's well drained, so we often add in some extra grit. It's a good idea to choose a pot that's not too big – just a couple of inches wider than the actual bulb – as amaryllis prefer being on the snug side.

We keep them in a shady part of the greenhouse until the flower bud starts shooting up, then arrange a covering of moss at the base before bringing them into the house. You do need to water them a fair amount, but they are worth it. They benefit from being in a spot that's well lit, and when they start to flower, I turn the pot regularly so they don't end up leaning towards the light – I find this keeps them nice and straight. The flowers are quite large and can become quite top heavy, so to stop them from toppling over, I put in a few sturdy twigs to help support the stem.

I keep my favourite amaryllis, 'Apple Blossom', in the greenhouse until the flower buds appear, then bring them into the house to enjoy.

Hyacinthus orientalis
(hyacinth)

I do love to have plants in the house, and in spring, I often grow hyacinths in pots as they are easy to grow and smell wonderful.

Leucojum
(snowflake)

Lunaria annua
'Chedglow' (honesty)

Hyacinthus orientalis (hyacinth)
I love to have things flowering in the house in spring, and I often plant hyacinths as they are easy and fun to grow and the scent is wonderful. Although they come in a range of colours, again my preference is for just the blue and white ones.

If I can get the multistem ones, all the better. I find the ordinary ones often vary too much in height, with one ending up at 8 inches (20 centimetres) and another at 4 inches (10 centimetres). Multistems seem more reliable and are a relatively good buy for the amount of flowers you get. If you do end up with the single ones rather than multistem, it's not a bad idea to grow them individually in pots and then move them into a group that works together height-wise.

For growing indoors, I buy the prepared bulbs, which have already been treated to a period of cold that encourages them into growth earlier than regular bulbs for the garden. I plant them in autumn in pots using multipurpose compost. I arrange the bulbs so that they aren't touching and the tips are just showing above the compost.

Importantly, I always put moss around the bulbs so they look neat. I generally find moss in my own garden or it can be sourced sustainably. If I need to stake the hyacinths, I simply use a few little twigs from the garden with twine to hold them up discreetly. I keep them in a bright, cool spot in the house, as if they get too warm, they can shoot up too quickly and become top heavy. I check them regularly to see if the compost feels too dry and water well when they need it.

Once they've finished flowering indoors, I plant them straight out in the garden. At Watercroft, I used to put them in our picking bed, and here in Henley, I put in a few rows of regular hyacinths at the back of the tennis court. I've also planted them in the garden proper and, I'm afraid, I've made mistakes here as I sort of dotted them here, there, and everywhere in a higgledy-piggledy fashion. So we pulled them up and put all the blue ones in a group and all the white ones together, so it looks a lot better.

Leucojum (snowflake)
The pure white, bell-shaped flowers of snowflakes are quite nice to pick for a spring display in the house. They look a bit like a giant snowdrop with stems around 20 inches (50 centimetres) tall. Like snowdrops, they are grown from bulbs that are best planted in the green (with leaves), just after flowering in March with their tips just above the surface of the soil. They like well-drained soil with plenty of moisture.

Lunaria annua 'Chedglow' (honesty)
This unusual honesty was suggested to me by garden designer Bunny Guinness and it's really good. It forms a low, bushy clump of heart-shaped leaves in dark chocolate-purple to green, and large, loose clusters of deep pink-purple flowers in late spring to early summer. It reaches about 36 inches (90 centimetres) tall. The seed pods are the usual flat, oval, translucent, silver-dollar type that you get with the more common variety of honesty. It's usually grown as a biennial, and in its second year, it may self-seed lightly around the garden.

Narcissus (daffodil)
I have a number of different daffodils around the garden and these are among my favourites. 'Rijnveld's Early Sensation' (12 inches/ 30 centimetres tall) is a warm yellow, compact, fairly ordinary-looking daffodil but a great joy as it comes so early. I also grow 'Bridal Crown' (14 inches/35 centimetres tall) with sweetly scented, small, creamy white double flowers in mid-spring.

For me, the very best of all is 'Silver Chimes' (12 inches/ 30 centimetres tall), which has creamy white petals around a pale yellow cup and a lovely scent. This is also a mid-season flowerer. I also love 'February Gold' (10 inches/25 centimetres tall), an old variety that has small, bright yellow flowers with darker trumpets a bit later, and 'Hawera', a diminutive variety (7 inches/18 centimetres tall) with recurved lemon-yellow flowers, which is later still.

The scent of Narcissus *'Silver Chimes' is fresh and strong.*

Spring

Omphalodes cappadocica
'All Summer Blues' (navelwort)

I find the bright blue flowers of Omphalodes *such a cheery sight – they can really brighten up a shady spot in the garden.*

Primroses are such a reminder of my childhood. I have always loved picking them and I fill the house with sprigs in little vases each spring.

Primula vulgaris
(primrose)

The soundest of all of them is 'Tête-à-tête', a dwarf variety with yellow petals and a deeper yellow, shallow trumpet. If you're buying daffodils for the first time and especially if you've got a small garden, I'd highly recommend 'Tête-à-tête'. It is just 8 inches (20 centimetres) tall, produces two to three small, bright yellow, trumpet-shaped flowers per head, and performs reliably each year.

I also like the dwarf variety called 'Toto', which is a creamy white daffodil with a pale yellow trumpet. It's 10 inches (25 centimetres) tall and flowers early in the season with three heads per stem.

It's well worth going through the catalogues and making a list of one's favourites. Some of them have a lovely, strong scent too. I like to plant several different sorts so that they come up in succession and I always have something to pick for the house.

Growing daffodils

Generally, daffodils are easy to grow. Some flower as early as January, while others flower as late as the start of May. They should be planted in autumn and do best in moist, well-drained soil, ideally in a sunny spot. If the soil is compacted, then I dig it over and sometimes add in some compost or well-rotted manure at the same time. Obviously, daffodils come in different sizes, but as a general rule, plant them about twice the depth of the bulb, or around 4 inches (10 centimetres) deep. Once the flowering period is over, I deadhead them, taking off all the flowers, but leave the foliage to die down naturally so the nutrients feed the bulb and keep it strong for the next year.

Omphalodes cappadocica 'All Summer Blues' (navelwort)
I've planted this *Omphalodes* in a little shady bed near the house. It's a lovely, little, low-growing perennial (about 8 inches/ 20 centimetres tall) with masses of cheerful, bright blue flowers in spring above a neat mound of mid-green foliage. They look a bit like forget-me-nots. I've had this for over three years now and it's really very good for somewhere that's shaded.

What I've realized over the years is that if you've got a shady area, don't try to go against it. Don't put anything there that needs

full sun just because there's a gap and you'd like it there. Positioning plants to suit their needs is very important.

This particular cultivar blooms a lot longer than others, usually from spring all the way through summer. *Omphalodes* also likes moisture-retentive soil, and you do have to watch out for slugs – it's good to surround the plant with grit to deter them. As with lots of my perennials, I deadhead all the time to encourage more flowers.

Primula vulgaris (primrose)
These pretty little plants always bring to mind childhood memories of picking them with my family and tying up little bunches with lengths of wool. They are native to the UK, and you can often spot their pale lemon-yellow flowers lighting up woodlands and beneath hedgerows. They are one of the first flowers of spring, and you can often have flowers from March to May.

They are easy to grow, producing a semi-evergreen rosette of bright green leaves, followed by clusters of flowers on individual stems up to 8 inches (20 centimetres) tall. Once established, we've found they will often self-seed gently around the garden. They like damp shade best of all.

I like to have little sprigs of them in small vases around the house, and as well as looking so charming, they are sweetly scented too. Although it's possible to grow them from seed, I don't, mainly because my daughter gives me primroses as she's got masses of them in her garden.

Tulipa (tulip)
One tulip that I absolutely love and always grow is 'Angélique'. It's a double tulip with lots of pale pink petals streaked with darker and lighter shades of pink, and as they age, there can be a green streak to them. They look a bit like a peony and are wonderful in vases around the house. They reach about 16 inches (40 centimetres) tall and flower a little later than most tulips, usually around April to

My favourtie tulip, 'Angélique', makes a lovely cut flower.

May time, but go on blooming for about eight weeks. Each year I buy a few more as they don't always come back strongly.

Another I'm keen on is 'Spring Green', which is an elegant Viridiflora-type tulip with pale creamy white petals and a wide, green streak up the centre ('Viridiflora' refers to this distinctive green marking). It reaches around 16 inches (40 centimetres) tall and usually flowers around May. They are relatively inexpensive too compared to some other tulips.

Another Viridiflora tulip I like is 'China Town', which is a soft pink colour with beautiful feathered green markings that rise up from the base of the petals. The greyish-green leaves are edged in white. It reaches about 12 inches (30 centimetres) tall and also flowers in May.

Growing tulips

Although tulips are technically perennial, many of them aren't that reliable, so I tend to replant more every year to make sure I always get a decent display. There are different flower shapes and lots of different colours too, so getting a mix that works together for a single display can be a bit tricky, but you can often find bulb mixes for sale. Ideally, I plant tulips in mid- to late autumn so that they can get going before winter. Also, the cold temperatures help to eradicate any diseases in the soil and prevent these from affecting the bulbs.

Most advice says that you should plant tulip bulbs at a depth twice the size of the bulbs, but I follow Sarah Raven's advice and put them in much deeper – more like three times the size of the bulb – as I believe it helps them come back the next year. Tulips do best in a sheltered, sunny spot with well-drained soil, ideally improved with compost or well-rotted organic matter.

Spring containers

In April, I'll often freshen up my winter pot displays by adding in some additional spring-flowering plants such as wallflowers, ideally in pale lemon or white. I use them to fill the gaps made when I take out the hellebores, which I replant in the garden.

If you want to include tulips, make sure the variety you choose is a suitable height for your container. If you've got a big container, you can have the taller ones, but if you put tall tulips in a small container, they'll simply fall over. I prefer to grow tulips on their own in pots as they don't really go with many other things.

I'm very keen on containers and the bigger the better, so if in doubt, choose the biggest pot you can.

A few years ago, I went to RHS Garden Wisley to have lunch with the then-curator, Matt Pottage. I wanted some inspiration for my pots, so we looked at lots of plants together. It's always helpful to go to a good plant nursery for inspiration, especially with someone knowledgeable.

I often try holding up various combinations to create a picture of how things could work together. I've tried all sorts of things in my pots and have recently tried using evergreen ferns. I find their texture works really well in combination with other things. Ferns benefit from a bit of feed from time to time in the growing season, so we make sure to do that to keep them healthy and strong.

My favourite pots
I'm very keen on containers and the bigger and better, so if in doubt, choose the biggest pot you can, and it's important to choose a good shape too. Little pots take too much attention and big pots are very, very rewarding. Bigger pots don't dry out as quickly as small ones, so you don't have to water them as often, and I've found it's always better to use a bigger container than a smaller one. Lucy, who works with me and is always by my side, loves vintage dolly tubs, which used to be washing tubs, and these are a decent size. If you want smaller pots, then I suggest grouping them together and buying a stand that allows you to put them in tiers.

Some people want to have these new tin containers. You can find all sorts of interesting things in antique shops and junkyards, and

I've even seen people using cattle troughs. We've got a lovely little nursery in Marlow, just up the road from here, called Danesfield, and they go all over the country finding interesting containers. They have cattle troughs, china sinks, milk churns – all different things and not too expensive.

I rather like terracotta and also great big copper pots. Personally, I don't like mixing different sorts of containers together and tend to stick with terracotta, as it's easier on the eye. Having a mix of different containers always reminds me of being on holiday in France, Portugal, or Spain, where you see people using lots of potted plants, often in old olive oil tins or so on. It's really charming but I don't think it translates to England.

I have a pet hate of coloured pots, but each to their own. Over the years, I've come to realize that whatever your taste is – be it terracotta, metal, or ceramic – it helps the overall look if you try to limit yourself to one type of pot. It makes everything look far more cohesive rather than having lots of different materials, which can be quite jarring.

Growing in pots

One of the great things about growing in pots is that you can move the plants around to different parts of the garden. Another good thing is that you don't need to totally redo them every season. I often leave things like the evergreen ferns or *Sarcococca* (sweet box) in place but will tidy them up if need be. However, it is good to scrape off a bit of the soil at the top and replace with some fresh soil.

Plants grown in pots are particularly susceptible to attack by vine weevils, so we check the plants and soil regularly, as well as lifting the pots up to see if any have hidden themselves away underneath. The adult weevils, which look like dark beetles up to about half an inch (10 millimetres) long, eat leaves, while the creamy white grubs attack the roots. They are fairly easy to pick off by hand, but if there are a lot of them, then I find it's worth emptying the pot out, removing as many as you can, and then repotting the whole thing with fresh compost.

With big pots, I invariably put chunks of broken polystyrene at the bottom, as it makes the pots lighter to move around and filling the entire pot is a waste of compost. Bunny Guinness recommends taking off the bottom of terracotta pots and putting them directly on the soil so that the plants can take root into the soil yet still look as if they are growing in a pot. We've done it with our bay trees, and the roots are now making their way down to the soil beneath. Obviously, when we do this, we don't put in polystyrene.

Buying spring bulbs

Spring bulbs are so lovely when it's cold. They are a sign that winter is over and a new season is beginning, so they cheer you up. I admit, I'm extravagant with bulbs, and I'll often buy in bulk with a couple of neighbours from somewhere like Parker's Wholesale. I get lots for myself and to give away to friends. I buy 'Angélique' tulips because they don't last that long so need replacing regularly. I also buy some early and late tulips and like to try out different ones.

I've found that it can be a false economy buying supposed bargains at the end of the season. Last year, I bought a lot of gladioli that were terribly cheap and planted them straight away. Although I got lots of foliage, I didn't get one flower. So I've left them in the ground, and it will be interesting to see if they flower at all next year.

I tend to buy bulbs from a catalogue from somewhere reputable, but if ever I buy at a nursery or garden centre, I look out for the ones that are plump and firm and avoid taking anything that is soft or looks a bit mouldy. I plant them in autumn, as it gives the bulbs a chance to get going before winter begins.

Q & A
Matthew Pottage

Over the years, I treasured my visits and chats with Matt when he was the curator at RHS Garden Wisley. He's a young man with so much knowledge and passion. I'm certainly going to try the lily of the valley with variegated foliage that Matt recommends. He also gives good advice for box replacements. I've used yew already but I'm tempted to try *Podocarpus nivalis* in the future.

What are your favourite plants for shade?

I love *Hosta* 'War Paint' for its wonderful, pleated leaves and memorable variegation; *Aspidistra elatior* 'Variegata' for a very dark, sheltered corner; and *Adiantum venustum* (evergreen maidenhair) for ground cover. Of course, it would be remiss of me not to mention *Cyclamen hederifolium*, the queen of shady borders and, in fact, dry shade too, where I find you simply cannot have too many. Something a little more special, which I treasure in a pot, is my variegated lily of the valley, *Convallaria majalis* 'Vic Pawlowski's Gold' – its foliage is simply sensational.

Do you have any favourite indoor plants that are easy to grow or maintain?

I have a soft spot for the elephant's foot plant, *Beaucarnea recurvata*, as it is so tolerant of neglect and looks so fascinating! For flowers, I think it's hard to beat the shaving brush plant, *Haemanthus albiflos*, which flowers annually in a cool, bright location. It's quick to multiply, so you can give bulbs away to friends!

Are there any new plants that you are particularly excited about growing?

I'm excited about the 2025 RHS Chelsea Flower Show Plant of the Year, *Philadelphus* 'Petite Perfume Pink', as it's unusual to see a mock orange with pink in the flower petals. It still has a brilliant scent like the old varieties and has a very elegant, arching habit with pretty, small leaves. Perfect for small spaces!

*Can you suggest a replacement for box (*Buxus*) due to problems with box blight and box tree caterpillar?*

Without a moment of hesitation, for me, it has to be *Podocarpus nivalis* (mountain totara) or any cultivars of that species. Just like box, it doesn't grow too fast, rejuvenates if pruned into old wood, can be struck from cuttings, and copes with both sun and shade. Of course, many *Lonicera* look the part, but they grow so quickly. They need several clips a year to keep them looking sharp, and I simply don't have the time!

What is your favourite gardening tool or piece of kit?

I find pruning a satisfying job, but only with a super-sharp, small folding saw to make very precise, clean cuts. I wouldn't be without my folding Silky saw. You can replace the blades as required, they slice like a hot knife through butter, and are adjustable into a couple of angles to reach the most awkward of branches.

Summer

June is when things really start to happen in our garden, with plants bursting into colour. We usually see the first flowers around mid-June. I always look forward to seeing the sweet peas growing up the canes and enjoy tying them in so they grow nice and straight.

We don't do No Mow May, as we have a section of the garden that we let grow wild and have so many flowers that help attract bees and other beneficial insects. June is when we cut back our wisteria to encourage a second flush of flowers – another great joy.

Sometimes I'm given some of those pretty miniature roses as a present for the house, but, really, they don't like being indoors. I recently tried trimming them right down and planting them beneath the 'Chandos Beauty' roses where I can enjoy them. I've found that as long as you water them, they bloom beautifully. It's the same with the pots of pansies I receive. The ones I put in the garden last year are ripping away and are a lovely reminder of the person who kindly gave them as a present.

> *If I do lose a plant, my children will say, 'Mum, what would you like? You're so difficult to buy for.' And I just say I'd love such and such, and give them the details of a particular plant that I want.*

Eating al fresco
I love to eat al fresco in summer, which is why I chose furniture that we can leave out. We have a table and chairs made of relatively heavy metal that I can move around. It's white, and in early summer,

I've had this elegant metal garden furniture for 30 years and it has never had to be repainted. I enjoy hosing it down in spring to remove any green sludge.

Aconitum
(monk's hood)

The pretty purplish blue blooms of monk's hood make for great long-lasting displays as cut flowers.

Agapanthus thrive in my garden. I cut them back regularly and I'm rewarded with lots of beautiful blue flowers throughout the summer.

Agapanthus
(African lily)

I use the pressure hose to clean it; it's very rewarding. I keep the cushions in the orangery hidden away in a wooden baker's proving bin that we've had for years. It was given to me by the Woodbridges Grocery & Bakery in Penn when it closed down. When the lid is shut, it doubles as a sideboard.

I always have pelargoniums in pots and it's nice to have those displayed on the table. After lunch, we often play a bit of croquet on the lawn.

Key summer plants

For me, gardening is about trying to get interest and colour all year round, and in summer, there are so many wonderful plants to choose from. I always like to have something to bring into the house, and over summer, there are always plenty of little bits and bobs to pick.

Summer is the most colourful time of year in the garden and as well as always growing some of my firm favourites, I still love to try out new plants. Over the summer months, if I'm free on a Sunday afternoon, I love to visit local gardens opened for the National Garden Scheme (NGS). The plant sales are irresistible, and as the gardens are local, I know that plants will grow in mine.

I must admit that I find it more of a challenge to get colour going into late summer and early autumn and really have to think about how to go about this. There aren't many bulbs in late summer, but hydrangeas are amazing for that time of year, and one of the great things about them is that they pick so well.

Here are some plants that I most highly recommend for June through to August.

Aconitum (monk's hood)
These beautiful perennials flower reliably, their purple-blue spires are good to pick, lasting well in a vase. It's a great plant for the back or middle of a border and does best in moist, well-drained soil in part shade. All parts of the plant are very poisonous so I'd recommend wearing gloves when handling them.

Agapanthus (African lily)
These are such a joy and grow well here. I like the blue and white ones best and their large, spherical flower heads bloom for ages. They have sturdy stems and the glossy, strappy leaves look good too. Not all agapanthus are hardy, although I've read that the herbaceous ones tend to be hardier than the evergreen types.

They grow between 2 to 3 feet (60 to 100 centimetres) tall, so it's good to take note of their heights if planting in the border, which is where I prefer to grow them, although they do grow well in pots too.

They like a sheltered, sunny spot and we always put a bit of grit in the planting hole before they go in. It's quite fun to keep the seed, although we've found that it can take a while for them to grow into proper plants. Usually we cut back the heads once they've finished flowering to keep them tidy and to encourage more flowers.

Alchemilla mollis (lady's mantle)
This is such a great little perennial plant with soft, green leaves and frothy, yellow flowers on wiry stems. It's relatively low growing – to about 20 inches (50 centimetres) tall – so it makes perfect ground cover. I cut it back towards the end of July, feed it, and keep it well watered, and it comes back and flourishes in a few weeks.

It's really easy to grow and spreads around, so there's never any need to buy any as you can invariably get spare plants from a gardening friend. It's tough too and will grow in numerous conditions. It looks really pretty in a vase with other things or just on its own.

Alstroemeria (Peruvian lily)
These are clump-forming perennials with long, dark green leaves and stems of exotic-looking flowers. They really are wonderful; the best thing ever. They are easy to grow, prolific, very floriferous, and make fantastic cut flowers as they last for ages.

We've planted our alstroemerias in the vegetable garden, and to make sure they grow nice and straight for picking, we've put four

Alchemilla mollis is great for ground cover and in flower arrangements.

Summer

posts around them with pig wire fixed to the top for them to grow through. We do have to water them a bit but that's all.

They flower from June through till November, and I find they are incredibly useful as I often take a bunch of the flowers when I meet up with friends. I pick them just before they come out and they last for ages – far longer than pretty much any other cut flower.

I'm growing a number of different ones, and I especially like the taller ones such as the Summer Paradise Series, including 'Indian Summer', which can grow to 30 inches (75 centimetres) tall. I find the tall ones far better as the longer stems work well in a vase.

Generally, I prefer them in pinks and whites and I am not so keen on the orange ones, although interestingly, they are the ones that are the most prolific.

I avoid buying plants that have 'Princess' in their name because they're squat and no good for picking. I once made a mistake and ended up with a couple of them so have learned my lesson. I think they must have been wrongly labelled as it said they grew to 12 inches (30 centimetres), and I thought, well, perhaps in my soil, they'll grow a bit more. Well, they didn't, so I'm going to move them to a border.

I like to start them off with decent-sized, tall plants. Like dahlias, they are tender when young and hardier when more established. I have bought alstroemerias as mail-order plants, but they were in 3½-inch (9-centimetre) pots, and it takes a long time for a 3½-inch pot to bulk up. I've also found them at rare-plant fairs, where they tend to have bigger plants.

It's best to plant them in a sheltered spot, either in full sun or part shade. We dig planting holes around 8 inches (20 centimetres) deep and 18–24 inches (45–60 centimetres) apart. We find it best to improve drainage by dropping a handful of grit into the hole before putting in the plant. Planting them deeply means they are less likely to be affected by frost, and to be doubly sure, we give them a good, thick layer of mulch over the winter. Being herbaceous, they go

This simple structure helps to keep our Alstroemeria *straight for picking. Sometimes I top the posts with pig-wire mesh.*

down to almost nothing over the winter, but as soon as the shoots come up, they are very likely to get frosted, so we cover them in fleece to protect them.

When picking alstroemerias, the experts say that it is important to pull up the whole stem rather than cutting it, so I always do this, using both hands to tug them so that the stems sort of disengage. Indeed, at the RHS Chelsea Flower Show in 2025, I was talking to the owner of Woburn Farm Plants, who are specialists in alstroemerias. They said to pick them, you just give the stalk a little twist as you would when picking rhubarb. I think it's very good advice. Removing whole stems helps make space for the new ones to grow. We've found that this is the best way to remove faded flowers too as it encourages the plant to put on more blooms.

Ammi majus (bishop's flower)
I bought these annuals as plug plants and planted them among the agapanthus. I think they look rather good and they seem to like it here. The contrast of the strappy agapanthus leaves works nicely against the airy, dainty, white umbels and fern-like foliage of *Ammi*.

To start them off by seed, they need to be sown in early spring, ideally directly into the ground. If that's not possible, you can start them off in pots and then transplant about four to six weeks after sowing. Once established, they seem to cope with dry spells. They self-seed quite nicely, and if we end up with too many, they are easy to pull up. They can grow to about 5 feet (1.5 metres) tall.

Anchusa azurea 'Loddon Royalist' (bugloss)
I keep growing this even though I have lost a few plants, and I'm not sure why as I've read that it tolerates all soils. It's such a good thing to have in summer. It has loose clusters of wonderful, intense, deep-blue flowers on strong stems that emerge from a rosette of mid-green leaves that are a bit hairy. The stems are tall (about 3 feet/1 metre) yet are sturdy enough that they don't need to be staked. It likes good drainage and full sun and is tolerant of drought. I will try again as I love the dense, deep blue flowers.

Ammi majus
(bishop's flower)

Anchusa azurea
'Loddon Royalist' (bugloss)

Argyranthemum
(marguerite)

Astrantia
(masterwort)

Argyranthemum (marguerite)

My friend Jenny Hopkirk kindly gave me some of her marguerites that she'd had for 20 years. They are relatively short, and although we don't know the exact name, there are several cultivars of short marguerites available, including Madeira Series, Grandaisy Series, and Beauty Series. I don't like those with long stems.

They are tender perennials and we propagate them in August, and I always say, 'It's time to take Jenny's cuttings.' They take as easy as pie so they work out very inexpensive. We plant them five to a little pot, and when they are a decent size, we pot them up individually.

We put them out in the garden in spring, and as they grow, we keep pinching them out so that they end up forming nice, bushy plants. We've now got them growing in large pots on the terrace, where they grow to at least 24 inches (60 centimetres) tall.

Astrantia (masterwort)

This is an easy-to-grow perennial with interesting flowers that have a domed centre (which looks a bit like an old-fashioned pincushion), surrounded by a ruff of small, pointed petals, which are technically called bracts. The green leaves are attractive too, and the long flower stems are nice and wiry, so we don't need to stake them. They grow to about 36 inches (90 centimetres) tall.

Astrantias are perfectly hardy, dying back over winter, then shooting back in spring and flowering from June to August. They come in a range of colours, including pale greenish white, pink, and wine red. I like the red ones best of all.

They seem to be happy in sun or light shade although they don't do well in deep shade. This is another plant that benefits greatly from deadheading, so we snip off spent flowers all summer long. One of the best things about astrantias is that slugs and snails ignore them.

Clematis 'Hagley Hybrid'

There's an almost overwhelming choice of clematis to choose from, so we always do our research and choose the right one for where we

Clematis 'Hagley Hybrid' thrives on our north-facing wall.

Summer

plan to grow it. We grew 'Hagley Hybrid' at Watercroft and now have it here at our garden in Henley.

It's a relatively compact, deciduous, perennial climber and flowers from mid-summer to early autumn, producing masses of large, pinkish flowers up to 6 inches (15 centimetres) across, which have a central tuft of dark red anthers. It's a pretty robust plant and grows vigorously in the right conditions to about 8 feet (2.5 metres) tall.

All clematis like to have their roots in shade, and we've found that this one is perfectly happy on a north-facing wall. The flowers tend to fade if they are in strong sunlight. As a rule, clematis are hungry and thirsty plants, so we water regularly and thoroughly and also feed just before flowering with tomato feed (one that is high in potash).

Clematis are divided into three different pruning groups, so you've got to learn which type you've got in order to know when to prune. This one is in group 3, which means it flowers on growth produced earlier in the same season, so according to the rule books, it should be pruned in late winter or early spring. It's a very easy plant; you just chop it to ground level at the end of the season.

Cosmos bipinnatus (cosmea)
With cosmos, I only like the dwarf ones such as the Sonata Series, which are all quite compact. They grow to about 16 inches (40 centimetres). They are annuals, very easy to grow from seed, and produce masses of large, daisy-like flowers from summer all the way through to autumn. They like to be in full sun.

I particularly like the pure white ones, but they come in lots of lovely colours, ranging from pinks and reds to chocolate and even a pale yellow one. The feathery, bright green foliage is attractive too. They look wonderful in the border and make a great cut flower.

Delphinium 'Molly Buchanan' (delphinium)
I have delphiniums for picking. I grow 'Molly Buchanan' as it's my favourite. I buy them from Blackmore & Langdon's, the delphinium specialist near Bristol. It's named after my late aunt, my mum's sister.

The tall spires of flowers are a glorious, intense blue with a dark, almost black eye at the centre.

They like a sheltered, sun-baked position, and before planting, we always dig in plenty of well-rotted manure or our homemade compost. The tall stems, which grow to about 5 feet (1.5 metres), must be staked otherwise they are in danger of collapsing over, and we do this early in the season using bamboo canes and twine. They usually flower from mid- to late summer, and I like to stake them well before they are fully grown as that way the stakes become hidden as the plants grow.

Delphiniums do tend to suffer from powdery mildew, so we don't plant them too closely as it's best if there's good air flow. The biggest problem we have with them is slugs and snails, which will strip plants to almost nothing overnight. We put a deep ring of gravel around the base of plants (we have plenty spare as we use it on the drive) and will also resort to slug pellets if need be. Blackmore & Langdon's claim that it's 'possibly the ultimate delphinium blue'.

Dianthus barbatus (sweet william)

We grow sweet william because they remind us of our son William, whom we lost. I've dedicated a whole bed to them, and they've been very successful both in the garden and as a cut flower, lasting for two or three weeks in a vase, far longer than most other flowers, so that is really good. They have a lovely, sweet scent and come in lots of pretty colours, although I generally prefer the red and white ones.

Technically, they are short-lived hardy perennials but are often grown as biennials. We grow them from seed, which we sow in spring, but you can also buy them as plants to be put in the ground in early autumn for flowers the following summer.

They are best grown in a sunny spot, and while they are getting established, we keep them well watered. After flowering, we cut the stems back to the ground to increase the chances of it coming back the next year. They reach about 16 to 24 inches (40 to 60 centimetres) tall.

Cosmos bipinnatus (*cosmea*)

Delphinium *'Molly Buchanan'* (*delphinium*)

Dianthus barbatus (*sweet william*)

Erigeron karvinskianus (*Mexican fleabane*)

Erigeron karvinskianus (Mexican fleabane)

I love this prolific, little low-growing daisy. It blooms profusely from around May until October, starting out pure white then gradually fading to pink. I remember seeing them at Salcombe in Devon, just at the side of the Fortescue Inn, where there's a whole flight of steps with them growing in every crevice. It looked wonderful.

One of the reasons I enjoy visiting gardens is that I'll often see things I rather like and want to have a go at copying them. I used to grow white trailing pelargoniums at the base of our lollipop bay trees, which are in huge pots. They were a chore to deadhead and I lost them over the winter. I've since replaced them with *Erigeron*, and they make a great show. We cut them back at the end of the season and they come back each year, growing to about 12 inches (30 centimetres) high.

Eucryphia

This is not one of my successes. I tried to grow this beautiful shrub in our last garden, and we have tried here and failed. I love the white, scented, cup-shaped flowers in late summer and fresh, dark green foliage. I have tried growing *E.* x *nymansensis* twice and they died. I now realize that they flower in acidic (ericaceous) soil, so now I'm inclined to grow them in pots in the correct soil.

Often, when you buy them, the plants aren't in great shape, so you've got to be bold and be prepared to prune in order to fully adapt and get a better form. I like encouraging it to sprout new growth from the inside, which I think looks so much better. Eucryphias do best in a sheltered position in the sunshine, and the shrub species grow to about 10 to 20 feet (3 to 6 metres) tall.

Geranium 'Rozanne' (cranesbill)

This beautiful, hardy, perennial geranium is exceptionally long flowering (from early summer through to late autumn), producing lots of intense, violet-blue flowers with dark purple veining and a white centre. The mid-green leaves are deeply lobed with a slight marbling.

It is vigorous, spreads easily, and is renowned for being easy to grow. It reaches about 24 inches (60 centimetres) in height. It responds really well to deadheading and is one of the longest flowering plants that I know of. It's what we might call a real 'doer'. 'Rozanne' doesn't mind terribly where it is planted and even does fine in shade. The only thing it's not keen on is waterlogged soil but there's no chance of that in our garden!

Geum

We have quite a few geums in the borders along the wall in the front garden, and I've bought a number of them from Clare Austin's nursery in Wales. One of my favourites is *Geum* 'Pink Petticoats', which has double, frilly-edged, pink flowers with a lemon-yellow centre. They're held on short, reddish-brown stems above a nice neat, little mound of mid-green foliage.

They grow to about 10 inches (25 centimetres). Geums are happy in full sun or light shade. They usually do well here, but I'm waiting to see if I've lost them in the summer drought when there was a hosepipe ban and they were just watered by hand.

Gladiolus

I've decided that I'm going to grow more gladioli. Their tall flower spikes are great for adding drama to a sunny border in late summer – they reach 2 to 4 feet (60 centimetres to 1.2 metres). They come in lots of different colours, everything from purple and magenta to yellow and white – my favourites are the pinks and whites.

We plant bulbs in late spring 4–6 inches (10–15 centimetres) deep, dropping some horticultural grit into the planting hole beforehand for good drainage. They like to be well watered during the growing season, and stake them before the flowers emerge.

I only grow the hardy varieties, as with tender ones, it's recommended that you lift the bulbs in autumn and overwinter, but I find that too time consuming. The hardier varieties are fine in frosty conditions, but it's always a good idea to cover them with a protective layer of mulch, just to be on the safe side.

Eucryphia

Geranium *'Rozanne' (cranesbill)*

Geum

Gladiolus

Heuchera 'Plum Pudding' (coral bells)

I've recently started to grow some heucheras and they spread well. I love those with dark leaves as I think they combine well with lots of other things in the garden and are useful for filling gaps.

'Plum Pudding' is a favourite and forms a neat mound of purple-plum leaves sprinkled with silver grey, which grows to about 26 inches (65 centimetres) high. As well as providing interesting foliage colour, shape, and texture, they produce wiry stems topped with airy sprays of little white flowers in summer. It's semi-evergreen so naturally loses some leaves in winter, but in autumn, we remove any of the foliage that look a bit worse for wear as then they look a bit tidier.

Hosta

If you've got a shady part of the garden, hostas are wonderful. They die back over winter, then nothing much happens at all until the end of May, when you have the excitement of seeing the new growth coming up. They make a great feature all summer and it's just so restful to look at them.

Hostas look wonderful in pots. I've not had much success growing them in the borders because the slugs love them, and it isn't pretty to see the damaged leaves. Where they have worked well is in a large, raised bed with a dry-stone retaining wall that we had built beneath a mature chestnut tree, which faces the orangery.

I had good advice from a wonderful chap called Chris Potts from Sienna Hosta, who's won numerous gold medals at RHS flower shows. He suggested that on top of the wall we have a flat stone that juts out slightly so that the slugs don't come up. It was built by Tony Shaw and he did a brilliant job. I keep an eye out for them, but usually they don't climb up, so it seems to work. As an extra deterrent, I spray the plants each week with a garlic solution recommended by Chris (see page 155). We find it works really well.

Heuchera 'Plum Pudding' has rich, plum-purple-coloured leaves.

The hostas do well in the raised bed we had built beneath a large chestnut tree. The dry-stone wall keeps slugs and snails away.

Hostas are not terribly fussy about what soil they grow in as long as it's relatively damp. That said, if it's too wet, they tend to die off, so drainage is important. We use masses of gravel – we have lots of it (grit is more usual) – around each plant and mulch the area with chipped bark, which helps retain moisture and looks smart.

We've grouped numerous different cultivars together so there's lots of shades of green and various textures and they look absolutely lovely there. I've even got them all labelled. They are underplanted with spring bulbs, and Chris has suggested putting wood anemones in there too, but I've decided that I prefer brunnera.

We have now added in some *Brunnera macrophylla* 'Jack Frost' (Siberian bugloss), a deciduous perennial with small, blue flowers in spring and heart-shaped, variegated green foliage in summer through to autumn, as it's very good in shade and no hassle. Around the outside of the stone wall I have planted spring- and autumn-flowering cyclamen (*Cyclamen coum* and *C. hederifolium*). Apart from watering them in dry spells, hostas don't seem to need much attention. In winter, we tidy away the dead leaves, and in late summer, because I don't like the flowers, I cut them off. For me, the hostas' beauty is in the leaves.

Hostas can also look wonderful in pots, and they make a lovely display for a totally shady, damp corner because, as woodland plants, that's what they like best. At Watercroft, we had a lot of them grouped together, with all different heights of pots – the bigger the better – and at the back we had some old chimney pots in which I would sit a plastic pot (that wouldn't drop to the bottom). I used a free-draining compost and topped it off with a really thick layer of gravel or shingle, making sure it sat just below the rim of the pot. That way you can water the plant without the soil spilling over. I used to put a saucer underneath each terracotta flower pot so that I didn't waste any water, and hostas like a lot of water anyway.

Some people put Vaseline round the pots to stop the slugs, but I've found they can't be bothered to climb up the sides, and I always watched like a hawk for slugs and snails. If I did spot any holes in the leaves, I would feel around with my fingers to find the culprit and pick them off.

Summer

....

Garlic spray

I like to use this homemade garlic spray to deter snails and slugs from eating my hostas. Place two whole bulbs of garlic in a saucepan containing 3½ pints (2 litres) of water, heat, and simmer it until the garlic bulbs are soft and squidgy. Remove the bulbs, mash them with a fork, then sieve into a bottle with a lid. It's dead easy. Then, when you want to use it, dilute 2 tablespoons of the solution in 8¾ pints (5 litres) of water and spray or water it over your hostas once a week.

Hydrangea arborescens 'Annabelle' (smooth hydrangea)
This is one of the very best hydrangeas and a sheer joy in the garden. It has a nice, upright habit, and in late summer, produces spectacular, huge white pom-poms, up to 12 inches (30 centimetres) wide, made up of lots of tiny, creamy white flowers. They like growing in sun to part shade, and we try to remember to water them a lot. Although they are hardy, the buds can get caught by a late frost, so we grow them in the front garden near the house where they have some protection.

The heads are quite heavy, so just before they flower, Kevin puts in shortened bean sticks (old runner bean sticks that are past their best) as supports and ties with jute twine. It takes time to put them in there, but it's worth it as you've only got to get a gust of wind and down they go.

'Annabelle' is one of the very best hydrangeas and a sheer joy in the garden.

This sort of hydrangea produces flowers on new wood, so we cut them right down after flowering and they come back beautifully. We interplant with tulips, which come up before the new foliage of the hydrangea emerges. I find 'Annabelle' doesn't last very well in a vase, but I know that some other hydrangeas do, and they look lovely just on their own.

In the autumn, I often buy white hydrangeas as houseplants, and they thrive if they are well watered, and they like to sit in a little water in the flower pot. As soon as they've had it, I cut them right down, stick them out outside in the greenhouse, and keep them watered until I plant them in the ground. It really works as you get to enjoy them in both the house and the garden – I don't like waste!

Hylotelephium (sedum, stonecrop)

There's lots of different sedums available – some are classified as *Hylotelephium* – and I love the way they go down to nothing in the winter and then just pop through and are beautiful from spring to late summer. The taller varieties are very good to pick and last for ages in a vase. That said, I tend to prefer the lower-growing, trailing ones, which make good ground-cover plants and have a nice way of tumbling over the edge of a wall or pot.

I particularly like the small-leafed ones. In fact, I can't resist them and have lots of different ones tucked away in the garden, which I put in little groups of three along the edge of the retaining wall at the garden entrance. They cover the ground, and it means I don't have to weed as much. When they get quite big, I split them in the autumn and put more along the wall's edge.

These little sedums don't take up much space, so you can put interesting things behind them. They prefer a sunny spot but will tolerate a bit of shade and are quite easy going. We just cut back old flower heads in spring as the new growth starts coming through.

One of my favourite low-growing sedums is *Hylotelephium cauticola* 'Coca-Cola'. It grows to about 8 inches (20 centimetres) tall and works well at the front of a border, in pots, and trailing over walls. It likes full sun and is exceptionally tolerant of drought. In late summer and autumn, it is covered in clusters of pretty, deep pink, star-shaped flowers. The fleshy, rounded, evergreen leaves, which are grey green with a tinge of pink, are also very attractive.

We grow Hydrangea *'Annabelle' next to the house in the front garden.*

Summer

Above *I find picking sweet peas regularly through the summer means that they keep producing more flowers.*

Opposite *I grow many varieties of sedum, including 'Coca-Cola'.*

Lathyrus (sweet pea)

I always grow sweet peas as they are easy to grow and perfect for cutting, producing flowers over a long season, usually from June to September. There is a huge range available, so we often try different ones to work out which colours and scent we like best. I tend to prefer the soft colours, including pinks, whites, and blues. Nowadays, I put in an awful lot more pink-flowered ones, because they never seem to flower as much as the other colours, although I don't know why. As a rule, I buy seed from expert grower Roger Parsons because he has a really good selection.

I've tried planting them in autumn and spring, but find we have the most success if we start them off in January. We sow ours in the greenhouse, but you could grow them on a well-lit windowsill. It's important to pinch out the tips when they reach about 4 inches (10 centimetres) tall so that the plants grow nice and bushy. We like to keep them short until we plant them outdoors somewhere sunny in early May, once there's no longer a risk of frost.

Most sweet peas grow to around 6½ feet (2 metres) tall, so we put three plants up one support. You can use bamboo or hazel poles (I like using hazel), and you can use the supports to form a wigwam shape or a long tunnel. Once they are in the ground, we put some fleece around the bottom of the sticks to protect the plants while they are young. They are quite tough, but I'm always a bit nervous having gone to the trouble of growing them from seed.

Lavandula angustifolia 'Hidcote' (English lavender)

If I'm honest, I've had more success with *Nepeta* (catmint) than with lavender. With lavender, it's important that you don't go into the old wood when you cut it back, and half the time, I miss the moment to do it and the plants end up leggy.

One lavender we have had success with is 'Hidcote'. For me, it's just as lavender should be, a beautiful lilac blue. Over the years, I've been given lavender as presents and sometimes people give me pink or white forms. I find they are a bit wishy-washy and the whole effect is spoiled. There's nothing quite like blue lavender.

'Hidcote' is a classic English lavender that forms a small, compact, bushy shrub with narrow, silver-grey, evergreen leaves and masses of deep blue-purple flower spikes that smell wonderful. It grows to about 24 inches (60 centimetres).

Lavender does best in a nice dry, sunny spot. Drainage is really important as they are prone to rot when overly wet. They can suffer in extreme cold, so it's worth throwing some horticultural fleece over them in winter to be on the safe side. Ideally, you prune lightly after flowering, cutting back the stalks of the flowers and about 1 inch (2.5 centimetres) of the growth made that year.

I make mistakes all the time. I put some lavender up against the wall behind our little box hedge, thinking it would do beautifully in a nice hot place. Sadly, it did nothing, so I replaced the plants and it did nothing again. So we put in some small agapanthus, which just romped away and look so much better. Maybe lavender likes to be away from a wall or perhaps the soil is too poor for it.

Lilium (lily)

I like lilies, but I have to admit that I tend to buy them without properly checking what eventual height they're going to grow. The ones I currently have are too tall and look hideous, but I haven't got the heart to get rid of them as they bravely come back every year. It's so important to study the heights of things, because you've only got to go around beautiful gardens such as at Eton College to see that everything is at the right height and the borders are really lovely.

I've got an orange one in the border, although I've no idea where it came from. It looks dreadful there but it's battled on and is huge. I wouldn't have bought that colour on purpose. Obviously, you can move plants when they're at the end of the season, but ideally, we'd get them in the right place from the outset.

I prefer white and pink lilies, and I like planting them in groups in the garden. If I can't find a suitable spot, I put them in big tubs for picking. Lilies are a great investment, as they are more reliable than other bulbs and do seem to come back each year in the border.

Lavandula angustifolia *'Hidcote'*
(English lavender)

Lilium
(lily)

Mandevilla sanderi
(Brazilian jasmine)

Nepeta
(catmint)

Mandevilla sanderi (Brazilian jasmine)
This tropical-looking climber has twining, woody stems, and spectacular, vibrant pink-red, trumpet-shaped flowers that are sweetly scented and simple, oval-shaped, glossy, evergreen leaves. Being tender, it's safest to grow indoors in plenty of sunlight and somewhere nice and humid, ideally a conservatory or heated greenhouse; I sometimes have it in the kitchen.

It likes loam-based compost and we add in some grit to help drainage. Water them as soon as the soil begins to dry out and feed during the growing season. Although in theory it's perennial, it's fast growing and people often grow it as an annual. To support my plants, which can grow to about 10 to 13 feet (3 to 4 metres), I use shortened bamboo canes.

Nepeta (catmint)
I really love catmint and find it's a really useful plant because it looks good for so long, flowering from summer to autumn. It likes being in a sunny spot and, once established, is pretty drought tolerant. When it starts looking past its best, if you just cut it down, new little shoots come up and it looks good again.

It's a good idea to cut back catmint in July, give it a good feed and water and then it will shoot back and look respectable. I get hold of the flower head and chop it right down. And I think it's well worth doing as you get a second flowering. I think so many things need tidying up, and it's amazing how they'll come back if you do it early enough and water it well. If it's happy, it will sometimes self-seed in any gaps.

While visiting Diana and Stephen Parker-Swift's lovely garden in Thurlestone, Devon, I admired the new bed of *Nepeta racemosa* 'Walker's Low' used as an edging plant. Inspired by how good it looked, I've put it all around the bed. It's been in a year now and it's triumphed. I cut it back after flowering, watered it generously, and it's come back. It has fresh, green, aromatic leaves and lovely, deep lilac-blue flowers from early summer to autumn, and grows to about 24 inches (60 centimetres).

Another catmint that I particularly like to grow is *N.* x *faassenii*, which has silvery, grey-green leaves and long stems of light violet-blue flowers from summer to early autumn. It reaches about 20 inches (50 centimetres) high.

We planted it at Watercroft, and after the first year, it didn't seem to be coming back. I poked my fingers down near the roots and I realized that there were slugs and they'd nipped off all the new little shoots, just as they do with delphiniums. I'm afraid I ended up putting slug pellets down, and low and behold, the catmint came back up. Now when I plant them, I put a bit of grit around the base of the stem, and they seem to battle through.

Oenothera lindheimeri (white gaura)

I love gaura, its starry flowers are really pretty and nice to pick for the house. It has a bushy habit, producing airy stems loaded with small, white flowers, often tinged with pink, over an exceptionally long period – early summer into autumn. The small, lance-shaped green leaves will often develop dark spots in lower temperatures, but this is nothing to be concerned about, and in autumn, the foliage turns shades of red.

I bought five plants at a garden show last year and planted them in the border at the front of the house, dutifully watered them, and looked after them, and they looked gorgeous and flowered for ages. But I left them out unprotected over the winter and unfortunately only one survived. I realize now that perhaps they are not completely hardy so do need protection when temperatures are exceptionally low.

I've divided the one I have got and am keeping the small plants somewhere very sheltered, at least until they get established. Gauras like a warm, sunny spot but can cope with some shade. Once established, gauras are fairly tolerant of dry conditions. Apparently, mature gauras do not like being moved, but you can divide and replant large clumps in spring.

My favourite gauras are 'Summer Emotions', which has white flowers edged in deep pink and grows to 36 inches (90 centimetres), and 'Gaudi Rose', which has deep pink flowers and reaches about 12 inches (30 centimetres) high.

Paeonia (peony)
We've got quite a lot of herbaceous peonies, and their sumptuous flowers are a joy despite being short flowering. For us, they usually flower in May or June and always add a bit of drama to the early summer borders. There's a really big range available, suitable for lots of different conditions, and they can flower any time from April through to July.

In fact, there are three types of peonies. Herbaceous ones tend to grow to around 36 inches (90 centimetres) tall then die back down to the ground each winter. Tree peonies have woody stems, can reach between 5 and 6½ feet (1.5 and 2 metres) tall, and are, in fact, deciduous shrubs. Then there's a group called intersectional peonies that is a cross between the two. Tree peonies are on my list to buy as I have space at the back of the borders, and I think they would look good there.

I particularly like herbaceous ones with single flowers in white, especially *Paeonia lactiflora* 'White Wings', which has pure white petals that splay out from a yellow centre. They reach about 32 inches (80 centimetres) tall, and I've read that they are more tolerant of shade than many others. There's also a very, very dark sort of winey red colour that's on my list but I'm not sure of the name. One year, one of the growers at the RHS Chelsea Flower Show who I'd talked to sent me a lovely unusual one with petals that look a bit like raspberry ripple.

I love picking peonies and putting them in a vase with nothing else. In fact, you don't need to arrange them – you can simply plonk them in the biggest pot you've got and they look absolutely stunning.

The best time to plant peonies is in autumn so they can get established before the growing season. We dig a large hole, drop the plant in so that the top sits around 2 inches (5 centimetres) below the surface, fill up with soil, and firm in place. We water in dry

Oenothera lindheimeri
(white gaura)

Paeonia lactifloria *'White Wings'*
(peony)

Pelargonium *'Sweet Mimosa'*
(geranium)

Penstemon

spells, especially in the first year. It's also good to water in dry spells in spring when the buds are forming. When I'm pruning, I take out the centre head, and with any luck, two buds will come either side and will flower.

Once when I went to Chelsea, I asked for advice from the peony stand. I said my peonies get sticky tops, the buds, and ants crawl all over them. Should I wash them or spray them or what should I do? They said do absolutely nothing, but they agreed that it's well worth deadheading and you should get more flowers.

I also asked for advice about the foliage, which I'm always tempted to cut back in August or September when it tends to get really dishevelled. Again, they said not to do it as, rather like daffodils, leaving the leaves on allows the goodness to go back into the plant and keeps them strong. It's a shame because they look dreadful, but we have to follow the gardening rules!

Pelargonium (geranium)
I've had scented geraniums for years. They are beautiful to look at with a really long flowering period – usually from May to October – smell lovely, and are relatively low maintenance. We like to have them in pots for summer colour, which we can move indoors or outside somewhere with lots of sunshine.

There's a large variety available in all different colours, but I like having just one colour or shades of the same colour and tend to have them mainly in pinks and whites. One of my favourites is *Pelargonium* 'Sweet Mimosa' – I've always kept those. They have clusters of pretty, little, pale pink, scented flowers and deeply lobed leaves that smell of balsam. I also like trailing ones, known as ivy-leaved geraniums,. They seem to be tougher and are good in pots.

As with all of our flowering perennials, we keep deadheading throughout the season to encourage ever more blooms. Pelargoniums are perennial but are tender, so they need to be kept somewhere frost free over winter. We cut them right back at the end of the year, pull off every leaf that's tatty, then put them in the greenhouse.

They look very sad and a bit dead while they are dormant over the winter, but as long as they've got a little bit of light, they start to bounce back in spring, which is when we start to feed them to really get them going. They do like a lot of feed, and we give them something like Tomorite, which is high in potassium. I'm told I mustn't be generous with it but follow the instructions, as too much doesn't do them any good.

If plants start to become a bit leggy, I chop them right back. It gets too hot for them in the greenhouse in the summer, so as soon as temperatures start rising, we bring all the pelargoniums outside again. In late summer, we cut plants right back, and if we take cuttings, we do so any time in summer. They are a great joy.

Penstemon

We have a number of penstemons in the garden. They are short-lived, herbaceous perennials, and I find them particularly good for adding late summer colour as their flowering season is exceptionally long. Some of them are not as hardy as others, so it's always worth asking for advice when buying them. The bright red ones and the strong-coloured ones seem to make more robust plants.

Penstemons can suffer in winter, but we do seem to be able to keep them, and if we take cuttings, we do that from late summer to autumn. In autumn, we also cut back about a third of the plant so it's got some leaves over the winter, then after the last frost in spring, we cut them back hard to get fresh, new growth. I have to admit that I once made a mistake and cut them back at the wrong time and I lost them. You must leave all the green on top and, with any luck, they'll come through the winter.

The penstemons that I find easiest to grow here include the deep wine-coloured *Penstemon* 'Garnet', the purply-blue 'Sour Grapes', and the soft pink 'Apple Blossom', which is my favourite. I bought some from Claire Austin's nursery, and they have tall stems and soft pink flowers with a white throat. They flower from June to September, and I've found that deadheading them greatly encourages more flowers to come back. The foliage is semi-evergreen so remains for most of the winter. It really is an impressive plant and reaches about 30 inches (75 centimetres) tall.

Phlox paniculata 'White Admiral' (perennial phlox)
I love all the phloxes, and there's a wide range to choose from – it's just a matter of selecting the colours, form, and height you like best. I think they are really useful plants as they are low maintenance and produce masses of flowers over a very long period.

One I'm particularly fond of is 'White Admiral', the perennial, herbaceous phlox that has an upright habit and reaches 36 inches (90 centimetres) tall. It produces masses of heavily scented, pure white flowers on upright stems and has attractive, lance-shaped, mid-green leaves. They grow quickly but are easily controlled by cutting back with shears. They like growing in full sun and respond well to a Chelsea chop in May as it encourages a lot more flowers in the season.

Plumbago auriculata (Cape leadwort)
My friend and neighbour Anne Eastick, who is a brilliant gardener, came with me to visit designer Bunny Guinness's garden near Peterborough. Bunny kindly gave us cuttings of this *Plumbago*, and I said, 'It's no good giving me a cutting as I'm not very good with them', so I gave it to Anne, who's far better at these things. She had great success and presented me with three little plants, and they've grown really well. I'm so grateful as they are such a joy.

Technically speaking, *Plumbago* is a shrub and reaches 13 feet (4 metres) tall. I keep ours under 5 feet (1.5 metres). It produces masses of sky-blue flowers from summer to autumn. There's nothing like *Plumbago*, but it is tender, so you've got to grow it where you can wrap it in fleece over winter, or grow it in a pot that you can bring into a conservatory or greenhouse as temperatures drop.

Prunus 'Kursar' (cherry)
According to Matt Pottage, who's now head of horticulture and landscape strategy for the Royal Parks, this early-flowering, small, deciduous cherry tree is far better than the more common

Above *This perennial phlox 'White Admiral' is beautifully scented and makes a really lovely cut flower.*

Opposite *I protect my* **Plumbago** *over winter to be rewarded with a mass of sky-blue flowers all summer.*

Prunus x *subhirtella* 'Autumnalis'. It produces a profusion of single, vivid pink flowers and has oval-shaped leaves, which start off a coppery colour and turn deep orange in autumn. The flaking bark is interesting too. It's fairly compact with a rounded shape and apparently, it's tolerant of pollution so good for those living in a city. It reaches about 13 feet (4 metres) tall.

***Prunus persica* 'Peregrine' (white peach)**
Homegrown peaches are far more delicious than anything you buy in the shops. We grow one tree, bought as an espalier, on a south-facing wall near the house. They like lots of sunshine in a nice sheltered spot. Before we planted it, we dug in lots of well-rotted manure and attached a series of wires to the wall ready to train it in.

Peaches blossom early in the year, often in March when there is still a risk we'll have frost, so we have to make sure that it is protected, otherwise we don't end up with any fruit, which would be rather sad.

There are few pollinators around so early in the year, so Kevin uses a little brush to hand pollinate. We had a special cover built, a frame with Perspex panels – a copy of the glass one at Wisley – that we can attach to the wall and dismantle when it's not needed. It's a complete indulgence but works really well. Alternatively, you could use a sheet of plastic attached to battens above and dropped to the ground, which is also very effective and far less expensive.

Once fruit starts forming, we thin them out to just one per cluster and feed with a fertilizer high in potash. We've had it in the garden for four years, and this year we harvested over 70 peaches, which has been a joy. As it's grown close to the wall, the soil tends to be dry so we keep it well watered. We prune it in late summer once fruiting is over, cutting back old branches as peaches only fruit on one-year-old growth. They can reach up to 20 feet (6 metres) tall but ours is cut to the height of the wall, about 5 feet (1.5 metres).

***Salvia* (sage, Balkan clary)**
Oh, I love salvias! They come in such beautiful colours and there are hundreds to choose from, but my absolute favourites are the

Prunus *'Kursar'*
(cherry)

Prunus persica *'Peregrine'*
(white peach)

Salvia farinacea
'Victoria Blue'

Stachys byzantina
'Silver Carpet' (lamb's ear)

dark blue ones. I love *Salvia patens*, which is such a lovely intense blue but, unfortunately, I had to give up on it because it's tender and needs to be dug up and brought indoors over winter.

I also like *S. farinacea* 'Victoria Blue', but that is also tender. The so-called perennial salvias, such as 'Amistad', 'Amethyst', and *S. nemorosa* 'Caradonna', are relatively hardy, but they don't like to be waterlogged and will suffer in extreme cold, so we like to put them somewhere relatively sheltered.

Many salvias are drought tolerant so don't need watering, and some of them will give a second flush of flowers if you cut them back after the first flowering. Don't cut back the foliage in autumn as leaving the leaves on helps to protect the plants over winter. Rather, chop them back to the ground in spring and the new shoots will appear. Just make sure they are not eaten by slugs.

We divide the salvias I like best in autumn and grow them on in the greenhouse so that we can have more of them. Salvias are really easy to take cuttings from, so we take lots in late summer.

'Amistad' is a particularly striking salvia and is relatively tall (4 feet/1.2 metres) with strong, upright, almost black stems, slender, green leaves, and large, tubular flowers in a beautiful rich deep purple. It is exceptionally long flowering and can bloom from late spring to mid-autumn if you keep on deadheading it. It's a half-hardy perennial, and in the right spot, will generally survive unless there's a really hard frost. I take lots of cuttings, which grow quickly and they make great presents for gardening friends.

I don't do much in the way of bedding plants, but *S. farinacea* 'Victoria' does very well. It's an easy-to-grow tender perennial usually grown as an annual. It produces lots of dark violet-blue flower spikes from summer to the first frosts. The leaves are narrow and fresh green in colour, and it reaches a height of about 20 inches (50 centimetres).

S. nemorosa 'Caradonna' is a very good, hardy herbaceous perennial. It forms a neat, dense mound of grey-green foliage and upright, purple-black stems with lots of stunning, violet-blue flowers. Again, it flowers from early summer until the first frosts and grows to about 24 inches (60 centimetres) tall.

Stachys byzantina 'Silver Carpet' (lamb's ear)

I love the rosettes of soft, silver-grey, evergreen foliage of lamb's ear but am less keen on the flowers, which I usually cut off. I've recently bought this cultivar to use as an edging plant as I heard that it rarely flowers, so it will be interesting to see how it performs. I'm trying to get it to grow along a low wall.

Plants grow to about 8 inches (20 centimetres) high with a spread of 18 inches (45 centimetres) so work well at the front of a border if there's a little gap. They form a dense carpet so are great for suppressing weeds. They do best in full sun and are drought tolerant.

Thalictrum (meadow rue)

My favourite *Thalictrum* are the pure white ones, such as *T. aquilegiifolium* 'Album', *T. delavayi* 'Album', and *T.* 'Splendide White'. These are all quite tall – around 5 feet (1.5 metres) – but because they are delicate, with slender stems, ferny leaves, and dainty flowers, they don't dominate. As well as the white ones, you can also find *Thalictrum* in acid green and lots of shades of purple.

Most species prefer a bit of shade, but they are fine in sun too. They don't like drying out, so we water them in dry spells, especially when they are still getting themselves established. Taller *Thalictrum* species are best in a more sheltered part of the garden at the back of the border, and we stake ours so that they don't lean over. If we don't want them to self-seed, then we nip off the flower heads, and after they've finished blooming, we chop down the stems.

Verbena bonariensis (Argentinian vervain, purple top)

This plant is really easy to grow and, if happy, will gently spread itself around. It reaches around 5 to 6½ feet (1.5 to 2 metres) tall and has wiry, branching stems topped with neat little clusters of lavender-purple flowers. The leaves are sparse, so although tall, it is quite transparent and really best suited to the back or middle of the border.

Unfortunately, it has self-seeded at the front of the bed, which makes it difficult to put in any other plant. When I first saw it

Thalictrum
(meadow rue)

Verbena bonariensis
(Argentinian vervain, purple top)

Verbena rigida
(slender vervain)

Veronica
(veronica, speedwell)

coming through, I was quite excited as I thought I recognized the leaves as *Verbena rigida*, and of course it wasn't, it was *V. bonariensis*.

It likes a sunny spot and flowers for a particularly long period – usually from June to September and sometimes even in October. It always self-seeds in our garden and we keep it to replant at the back of the borders.

Verbena rigida (slender vervain)
I'm very fond of this neat, low-growing verbena, which reaches no more than just 4 inches (10 centimetres) tall in our garden. It has lots of bright purple flowers all summer long and into autumn. It's a herbaceous perennial, although not fully hardy, so it dies back in winter and appears again in May to June in our garden with any luck. It usually overwinters so I'm hoping that I will get more of them appearing. It's a bit tender so does best somewhere sunny that doesn't get overly wet in winter.

Veronica (veronica, speedwell)
Veronicas are useful plants in the garden and have a reputation for being hardy, long lived, needing very little maintenance, and generally free of pests and diseases. In fact, there are three groups of veronicas: herbaceous perennials, dwarf, and moisture-loving, ranging in height from 1 to 4 feet (30 centimetres to 1.2 metres).

I particularly like the dwarf veronicas, which have masses of slender little spires, and find them a useful plant for the front of borders and as ground cover. We've got several varieties, and I like the blue and white ones best. Some flower in late spring but mostly they flower all summer and into autumn. As a rule, veronicas are happy in either sun or partial shade. Once they've flowered, trim and feed, and with any luck, they will come back into flower again.

Wisteria
We've had wisteria in Watercroft and Henley and what they like best is sun, so a south-facing wall is ideal, although we actually had one facing west and it grew there quite well. In my opinion,

Opposite *Our wisteria in full bloom.*

Above *My husband, Paul, kept the wisteria from covering the back door at Watercroft.*

the most beautiful wisterias are the ones with deep blue flowers, and the white ones are good for arches and tunnels. Personally, I think wisteria are never as good in pink, which I find a bit wishy-washy.

They are, in fact, climbing shrubs with deciduous, beautiful, highly scented, pendent flowers in May or June. Usually, the long panicles are packed with single flowers, but you can also get double flowered ones too, which is good. In autumn, wisteria produce pea-like seed pods and the leaves turn a good colour. The woody stems are very strong and can grow as thick as a small tree trunk, so we train ours up the house and support it with wires fixed to the wall.

We prune in February and again in August and feed with a high-potash fertilizer in the growing season, as they are hungry plants.

I've heard people complain that their wisteria doesn't flower, but they need to be established for at least four years before they really get going. It's worth being patient. I am told that it is best to buy them in flower so you are sure of the colour you're getting. This year was truly disappointing as pigeons nested in the wisteria and stripped the buds off many of the flower trusses.

Zinnia

I always like to grow zinnias as they are good in a jug and come in lots of rich, vibrant colours. They are mostly half-hardy annuals, but rather than grow from seed, I tend to buy plug plants from Sarah Raven, planting them in the ground in May. I'm not great with seeds so plugs are perfect for me.

The first time I did this, they didn't do well to start with, and I began wondering why on earth I'd bothered. Then, just before I went on holiday, I snipped off all the heads, and when I came back, they had really shot up and there were loads of flowers. I really like to pick them and they've done me proud.

I grow zinnias for cutting and they attract pollinators too.

Summer

If growing from seed, then either start them off indoors in March to April, planting them out in May to June, or sow directly in the ground in May. Generally, they flower from late summer through to autumn, after which I dig them up. One year, I bought too many of the green-coloured zinnias, so now I always buy more of the brightly coloured ones as I think a mix of different colours looks far better. Depending on the variety you choose, zinnias range in height with most of them reaching between 12 and 30 inches (30 and 75 centimetres) tall.

Our roses

We grow one colour and a variety of roses in beds on their own. I absolutely love them and people always comment on them. They really are a joy. So many people look at our roses and say, 'Oh, but we can't grow those.' As long as you've got suitable soil (not too sandy), and the right rose for your particular conditions, pretty much anyone can grow roses if they look after them, but for real success, they need lots of love and care.

There are, of course, hundreds of roses to choose from, everything from small shrubs to climbers or ramblers. As ever, you've got to do your research and find out how it will grow, the best position, and how scented it is, but there's a rose for any situation.

Most do best in an open, sunny spot, but there's one rose, a vigorous, pink, repeat-flowering climber called 'Compassion', that will do well on a north-facing wall, and we have grown it with great success. I would always advise choosing a repeat-flowering rose and obviously something that is less prone to pests and diseases.

Roses like to be planted in good-quality soil, so before planting, we add in at least a bucketful of well-rotted manure as well as Rootgrow for good measure.

Our roses get lots of care but I love them and they are definitely worth it!

The apricot-pink flowers of 'Chandos Beauty' are simply divine. I love to pick the flowers as much for their intoxicating scent and dark green foliage.

Caring for roses

To get the very best results, I have learned that roses like to be planted in good-quality soil, so before planting, we add in at least a bucketful of well-rotted horse manure as well as Rootgrow (mycorrhizal fungi) for good measure. I have a leaky hose on a controlled timer, which I use overnight when need be, but this is my extravagance. We water and feed them well twice a year – once in spring and then again after flowering – with a dedicated rose feed during the growing season, and it makes the colours become brighter. We also use chicken pellets fertilizer, which are relatively expensive but work.

It's important to watch out for greenfly, and if we spot it, we spray them. I would never spray vegetables, I wouldn't dream of that, but I do with the roses. At the end of the season, they can get a bit of black spot. I try to avoid them falling to the ground and put on gloves, pick off the affected leaves, and burn them or put them in the non-recycling bin. Definitely don't put them on the compost heap as they can spread the disease in the garden.

My husband, Paul, deadheads the roses diligently. He deadheads all through the summer and we find that it really encourages more flowers. Around mid-July, after a lot of deadheading, we feed the repeat-flowering hybrid tea and floribunda roses for more flowers in August to September.

When every head has gone, usually around the end of November, I cut the rose right down so that it is about 30 inches (75 centimetres) from the ground. We feed it, and it grows back and the results are wonderful.

Rosa 'Chandos Beauty'

When I was first choosing roses, I went to Harkness Roses nursery in Hitchin, Hertfordshire. I could see that their roses were all healthy and disease free. I really like their selection, they're British grown and the catalogue is full of excellent descriptions and information.

Regular deadheading encourages more blooms on our roses.

Q & A
Philip Harkness

Philip Harkness runs the family rose business Harkness Roses, founded more than 140 years ago, and has years of knowledge and expertise. Our large bed of 'Chandos Beauty' is a real feature in our garden.

What is your advice on planting roses?

A simple question that probably has no simple answer! Planting in well-prepared soil has a profound effect on the success of the plant. Roses love food. Adding compost or well-rotted manure helps the soil. The soil should crumble easily – if it stays in chunks and lumps, more compost, please. The soil is the foundation for the plant.

With good soil planting is easy. Dig a hole, put the plant in (to the right depth), and use plenty of weight to tread it in. It needs to be snug as roots need good soil contact to extract water and food. Loose planting fails. Water it in and keep watering in dry spells.

What are the advantages and disadvantages of buying pot-grown and bare-root roses?

Until the 1970s, about 90 per cent of all roses were planted as bare-root plants, resulting in at least 95 per cent success. A bare-root plant is dug from a field in autumn and despatched to the customer. The union (the joint of stems and roots) determines the correct planting depth. It should be at or above ground level.

Pot-grown roses can be planted all year. In summer, you take a root ball out of the pot and into your garden. Theoretically, the plant transfers to the new position without disturbing the roots. It takes time for the compost to bind with the garden soil and transfer water to the roots. Use the weather to guide you in watering. When it's hot and windy, water every day if it was planted within the last month. If it's cool and wet, water only once a week.

And the winner? A dead heat. Bare root wins in terms of cost and environmental impact, and pot grown wins on convenience. Both give equally good results when planted with love.

Can you grow rose shrubs in pots or should they be in the ground?

Yes, they can be beautiful in pots. The bigger the plant, the larger the pot should be. For a plant 5 feet (1.5 metres) tall, a 30-inch (75-centimetre) pot is the minimum. Growing in a pot shortens the life of the plant to six to nine years. In hot periods, they need copious amounts of water at peak times, while flowering. Always water pots in the morning: it is when the sun is out that they need the water.

Is it advantageous when planting a rose to use Rootgrow?

Rootgrow is mycorrhizal fungi. A population of these fungi aids the development of the roses' feeding roots. It is especially useful when you are planting a rose in soil where roses were previously grown.

What's your view on rose pruning methods and how often should pruning be done?

Pruning is a simple task complicated by overthinking and an excess of expert opinion. In nature, pruning is carried out by fire, frost, horses, deer, and other herbivores. Roses thrive in the wild, despite no manuals to advise the animals of the correct procedure.

Know what you are trying to achieve: a healthy, strong, bushy plant with plenty of blooms. Cut out dead, diseased, damaged, or weak growth. No pruning means a tall and leggy plant growing from the top and waving about in the wind. It's a weak plant.

On bush roses, prune last year's growth back by 50 to 75 per cent. Modern roses make so many stems, there is no need to look for an 'outward-facing eye' as all the old books suggest.

Trim and tidy in autumn. Prune in early March in south England and in late March in Scotland. It is almost impossible to damage the plants. Any pruning is better than no pruning, so give it a go.

What is your favourite gardening tool or piece of kit?

My secateurs. They fit like a glove. Another pair feels wrong, even if it's an identical pair of the same make.

Philip Harkness wrote that of all the roses he grows, the repeat-flowering hybrid tea *Rosa* 'Chandos Beauty' was the most successful, with the healthiest growth, best smell, and shiniest foliage, and he's right. In the printed Harkness catalogue, there's a brilliant system of marking each rose out of 10 for foliage, smell, and health, and 'Chandos Beauty' is a 10 in all three.

It really is an exceptional rose and produces masses of beautiful, strongly scented, pale apricot-whitish flowers that bloom from around June until the first frost – such a robust and successful rose. We grew it in the courtyard at Watercroft and it was much admired.

It grows to around 4 feet (1.2 metres) tall with a spread of 24 inches (60 centimetres). I like it so much that, in fact, I've planted more here in our current garden. We've also got a little block near the gates where people drive in, which is lovely, and a bank at the back of the house where they can be seen from the kitchen.

They are planted closer together than is recommended, but we feed and water them, and I'm happy with how well they are growing. They flower profusely and I pick bunches of them as I love the smell of roses. They look lovely in a vase and last about a week.

Climbing roses

I love having climbers along walls, although I don't think I'm particularly good with them. It's really a case of working out where I want to put one, the sort of height I want it to reach, and then look for something with good colour, scent, and disease resistance. If you want to grow your rose over arches and other sorts of supports, make sure that you choose a rose that will grow to a suitable height and isn't too prolific.

In both of our previous houses, we have enjoyed 'Graham Thomas'. We grew it as a short climbing rose, and its large, yellow flowers have a good fragrance, blooming repeatedly from early summer to autumn. Others I'd like to have if I had more room to

I grow 'Chandos Beauty' at the back of the house and, as I step out into the garden, I find their scent is as impressive as their blooms.

Summer

grow them would be 'Rambling Rector', 'Kiftsgate', 'Paul's Himalayan Musk', 'Gertrude Jekyll', and 'Compassion'.

'Paul's Himalayan Musk' is a rambler and produces sprays of little, pale pink, double flowers with a strong musky smell. It flowers in summer but just once, and it is renowned for being healthy. They look wonderful but you've got to have a sizable garden as it goes wild and loves climbing through bare branches.

Another to enjoy, if I had room, is 'Rambling Rector'. We also like 'Graham Thomas' very much. We grow it as an upright climbing rose, and it has rich yellow, double flowers that are lightly scented. It doesn't get too tall and is relatively disease resistant. It repeat flowers from early summer to late autumn.

The famous rosarian David Austin said that one rose you should not be without is 'New Dawn'. It's an old-fashioned, climbing rose that flowers prolifically from July to September and is said to be reliable and vigorous. The clusters of pale pink, semi-double blooms look wonderful against the glossy green leaves. They have a lovely scent too. Apparently, it's fine in sun and part shade.

Pruning roses
To improve their health, vitality, shape, and life span it is vital to prune roses. Most roses should be pruned in late winter to very early spring, apart from ramblers, which are best pruned immediately after they have flowered in summer.

The principle behind pruning, I have learned, is to remove any dead, diseased, or damaged wood, making sure to cut just above an outward-facing bud as this encourages the stems to grow outwards rather than in on themselves. If plants become congested, it discourages the free flow of air, which, in turn, can lead to problems with pests and diseases.

It's also good to cut any stems that rub against each other or are competing for space, as well as anything weak looking and spindly. Mum Block, my first gardening guru (the mother of my gardening friend Penny), told me to cut out anything that's less thick than a pencil's width.

Cutting main stems encourages fresh, new growth, and often when we do our final pruning of our 'Chandos Beauty' roses in March, we prune hard, cutting back to about a foot (30 centimetres) using sharp secateurs. In summer, we prune immediately after flowering but this time not too harshly. This system works for us.

Summer containers

It's such fun putting together pot displays for summer. I never do them until the end of May because there's a chance that a late frost might get them. I particularly like trailing geraniums, which do exceptionally well, and in between those I often have some tiny *Erigeron* daisies, which, once established, self-seed everywhere.

Planting in pots

When planting up pots, I like choosing particular colour combinations, and I usually aim for something a little bit taller in the middle and something that trails down over the sides, and then pack the plants in. I tend to overplant, but it makes the pots look generous, which I like.

I have always put crocks in the bottom because I was told to, but I'm not sure if it does any good. If they're very, very deep pots and your plants are not going to the bottom, I sometimes put in crumbled-up polystyrene because the compost is expensive, and it seems wasteful to fill it up unnecessarily. I always start them off with new, good-quality general-purpose, peat-free compost. I find it needs more feed than peat-based compost so we make sure to feed plants as and when needed.

I never fill the pot absolutely to the top because then there's no room for the water and I like to put shingle, gravel, or grit on top. For trees like bay trees, you can put a mulch of bark. It makes them look smart and helps retain the water.

When I'm going around a nursery with a trolley, I sort of arrange the plants in the top of the trolley, thinking how they might work. I don't go for bright reds and oranges and so forth. I always do the softer colours because that's what I like. Sometimes, I have them

Above *I like to overplant my containers as I prefer them to look really full and abundant. Here, I've used a mix of purple and white annuals.*

Opposite *'Frank Headley' variegated pelargonium is a great favourite of mine.*

all one colour, and it's such fun, putting plants such as nemesias and trailing geraniums together.

Once I've selected my plants and the pots are filled with compost, then I just arrange everything as if I were arranging a bowl of flowers and is pleasing to the eye. To my mind, the arrangement has to be symmetrical.

When the rain comes, I remind myself that it is not enough water, as when a pot is full of plants, it just runs off the leaves. Watering pots well is one of the secrets of their success, so we never let them dry out. Also I pick off any damaged leaves and deadhead to encourage more flowers. That said, I have given up on petunias as, lovely as they are, for me, they take up too much time to deadhead.

I'm afraid I tend to have the pots for just one season and then they've had it, but it means you can have the joy of replanting them again and again. I do keep pelargoniums over winter, covered with a fleece in the greenhouse at 46°F (8°C), cutting them back in spring and again in autumn.

With pots, I plant everything closer together than you're supposed to, water them well, deadhead, and feed all the way through the season, and I have great success.

Our herb and vegetable garden

In the last house, Watercroft, we had a big vegetable garden that produced lots of veg. I learned that it's important to keep reminding myself to grow what we like to eat. Since the children left home, we don't need to grow as much, and our new garden, which is much smaller, provides plenty for us.

Previously, we'd grow potatoes, but while they are easy, you do need to manage the timings. Often, we'd have to harvest them too late when they were really cheap to buy in the shops. I've never grown peas as you really have to be there to pick them at the right time, although I have tried sugar snaps, which were rather fun.

We now have raised beds built from brick in the vegetable garden and they have been a great success. It means it's easier to improve the soil and keep the vegetable garden neat and tidy, and for me, it's great to be able to sit on the wall for weeding. It makes harvesting crops such as strawberries a bit easier too.

I have friends who have allotments, and one of the joys of these spaces is making friends and sharing plants and gardening tips.

Growing herbs, fruit, and vegetables
I only have plants that are easy to grow as I don't want the faff of tricky things and I never want to spray plants we're going to eat. When growing herbs, fruit, and vegetables, the most important thing to consider is what you enjoy eating, and having a smaller garden makes you focus on what you really enjoy. It's also worth thinking about growing things that are expensive to buy or difficult to find, such as particular varieties of tomato or asparagus.

I like to grow herbs to use in cooking, including mint, thyme, dill, chives, and basil. I do wonder why would anyone ever buy mint if they've got a garden? It's so easy and spreads. For thyme, I recommend growing the broadleaf variety as it's easier to pick and chop.

Chives are another plant I wouldn't be without. I like to use some of the flowers in salads. They are easy to care for, I simply take sections of it, cut it right back, feed it, water it, and then it comes back up within 10 days. With French tarragon, we bring it into the greenhouse over winter so that it doesn't get damaged by the frost.

Growing your own veg means you can experiment with new varieties, and some things, such as garlic, are simply fun to grow. It always seems very strange that you plant garlic in November, but that's what you're supposed to do. We grow elephant garlic, which produces large bulbs.

To start plants off, these days I often grow from plugs as it takes the stress out of growing things from seed. Another thing I've

learned over the years is to concentrate on growing things that grow well in my garden's conditions.

Generally, we grow carrots, beetroot, perpetual spinach, banana shallots, purple or white sprouting broccoli, and sweetcorn if we have any space. No cabbage or cauliflower for me, we haven't the space.

I recently tried growing Kalette (flower sprouts), a cross between kale and Brussels sprouts, which produces small, edible buds on an enormous stem. It was initially attacked by cabbage white caterpillars, but we picked them off and threw a mesh over the top of the plants to prevent further attack. Kalettes are harvested in late summer and are delicious – less bitter than kale.

If you want to grow perennial crops, such as asparagus, you have to be prepared to give up a section of the garden and know that you have to wait for three years before the crowns are ready for harvesting for the first time. We put asparagus in as soon as we moved house, making sure the soil was in a good state. While we waited for them to be ready to pick, I made sure to keep the area free of weeds to give them the best chance of growing well. It's like cooking recipes: there are rules that you must follow, but it's so easy not to follow them.

I'm always learning new tips and tricks. For instance, if you grow carrots in a raised bed, they are less likely to get carrot fly. Also, planting rocket seeds after August avoids it being attacked by flea beetles, as they reduce as the temperatures drop.

Asparagus
It's such a treat to eat fresh asparagus straight from the garden in early summer. We eat it simply with butter or hollandaise sauce. We put in a bed of asparagus not long after we moved in, but it has not been a great success. I was originally inspired by going round the gardens at Bledlow Manor House in the Chilterns, owned by Lord Carrington, where, after years of having compost added, the bed had become raised up and the asparagus was growing in big, thick stems. I was envious, so that's what I'm attempting to create here.

Basil grows well in raised beds. I snip off the tops to stop the plant going to seed.

As asparagus is perennial, it's really important to start off with a weed-free area and keep it regularly weeded so nothing competes for nutrients and light. We grew ours from bare-root crowns, which we kept well watered while they were getting established and waited for three years before we made our first harvest. Textbooks say that if asparagus is harvested before that, it weakens the plant.

To harvest them, we use a sharp knife and cut the stems ¾ to 1¼ inches (2 to 3 centimetres) below the surface of the soil. I've read that it's best not to harvest after mid-June as that way the plants can build up their strength. At the end of the growing season, it's just a matter of cutting off the ferny foliage down to 4 inches (10 centimetres) above the soil and mulching with a thick layer of well-rotted compost. I'm disappointed with our asparagus bed. We still get a small crop and very few thick stems, but we enjoy it.

Picking asparagus

When our asparagus comes into season and I start harvesting it, I pick just a little each day. I cut it or snap off the stem where it breaks, then stand it in a jug of cold water in the fridge, adding more water as it grows. That way, it lasts two weeks. I see that our excellent butcher in Henley stands his bunches in water outside the shop to keep them fresh.

Basil

This is a really useful annual herb, and I grow sweet basil with large leaves each year and harvest it all summer. It's good with tomatoes, salads, and for making pesto. Depending on where you live, you can sow seed from spring all through to summer to have a continuous supply, but I generally sow mine in May.

We start it off in seed trays of multipurpose compost, and when it's big enough, transplant it into individual pots. We also do a row in the raised beds. To make them nice and bushy, we pinch out the tips and plant out in June. They like a sheltered spot in full sun, but

I use a knife or secateurs to harvest asparagus, cutting just below the soil's surface.

they don't like to be exposed to too much strong midday sun as their leaves are prone to getting scorched.

Although we do water our plants regularly, taking care not to splash the leaves to prevent fungal diseases and leaf spot, we don't overdo it, as basil suffers if it sits in very wet soil. The plants seem to go to seed quickly, so I pinch out the flower heads, which helps to encourage plants to become bushier.

Beetroot
This vegetable is exceedingly easy to grow, and because we like eating lots of it, we sow three batches of it over the season. We direct sow our beetroot seeds sometime between mid-April and June in shallow drills, ½ inch (1 centimetre) deep and about 4 inches (10 centimetres) apart.

During the growing season, we are vigilant and make sure to keep the area free of weeds, as well as watering regularly. They are usually ready to harvest after about eight to 10 weeks. When the beetroot is the size of a tangerine, I pull them up and cut off the leaves, leaving about 4 inches (10 centimetres) of stem above the beetroot, otherwise it bleeds.

I simmer them in water until tender, then drop them into cold water and peel off the skin, which comes off easily when they are cooked. Then I slice them and layer them in a plastic box with a lid, seasoning with pepper, salt, sugar, and vinegar. They keep like this in the fridge for three to four weeks. When I cook the next batch of beetroot, I use the same vinegar but boil it up to be on the safe side and add in more pepper, salt, and sugar to taste.

There's quite a range of different beetroot, including the commonly available dark purple ones to orange, yellow, and pink types. I usually grow 'Boltardy', a popular variety that is said to be bolt resistant, but one year we tried 'Chioggia', which has-pink skin that, when cut, reveals interesting white and red rings inside. I was really disappointed that the colours fade when you cook 'Chioggia', so now I just grow a few of these that we can slice finely and eat raw in salads.

Basil

Beetroot 'Chioggia'

Carrots

Celeriac

Carrots
One of the main problems with carrots is attack by carrot root fly, which makes them inedible. Fortunately, we manage to grow them well because having raised beds means that the carrot root fly (which only fly at a certain height) can't reach them. I know that some people cover plants with a fine mesh as this stops them too.

Carrots like plenty of sunlight and the state of the soil is also very important. We dig it over, breaking up clods of earth and removing stones. We sow the seed finely in shallow drills, any time from March to June, cover with a fine layer of soil, then water carefully to avoid disturbing the seed too much. After that it's just a matter of keeping on top of the weeds and watering in very dry spells. Carrots are very drought resistant, so they don't need too much in the way of watering.

I read that it's best to avoid thinning out carrots as the carrot root fly is attracted by the smell, which is why we sow seed sparsely. We make four sowings over the course of the season, and they generally take around 10 to 16 weeks before they are ready to harvest.

Celeriac
This is a strange-looking, knobbly root vegetable, but it's very hardy and you can leave it in the ground all through the winter and just harvest it when you need it. We grow celeriac from plug plants, which makes things easier. They have a long growing season – at least six months – so the earlier you start plants off, the better. We transplant in spring once there is no chance of frost. Celeriac does fine in either a sunny or slightly shady spot and they like to be kept damp, so we water them loads. We usually start harvesting them around October.

It's good in soup, with potato mash, or made into remoulade. My favourite way of cooking celeriac is as a purée. Boil cubes of celeriac in salted water until they are tender, drain off the water, then purée in a food processor or use a hand blender, and add full-fat crème fraîche along with pepper and salt to taste. It reheats well if covered in foil and put in a moderate oven for 20 minutes or so. If there is any left over, then it's wonderful added to soups.

Chives

This herb is really easy to grow. Chives have a mild onion taste that is useful as a garnish sprinkled over things like salads and soup, and they also work particularly well with egg, cheese, chicken, or fish dishes. The pink-lilac flowers are pretty too and can be used as edible decoration. I particularly like the broad-leaved variety, which has thin, strappy leaves.

It is a herbaceous perennial, dying back each year, but seems to return reliably year after year for us. You can start it off as shop-bought plants or grow it from seed. They seem to like well-drained soil in sun best but are also happy in part shade. You can grow them in a large pot but they prefer being in the ground. To harvest them, I simply snip off some of the leaves at the base and use them as fresh as possible.

Courgettes

This is another vegetable that's really easy to grow. Usually, I buy small plants that I put straight in the ground and then keep an eye out for slugs as they love to eat young plants. You can also sow seed indoors in trays in April or May, pot them on when they are big enough, and plant out when there's no longer a risk of frost, or direct sow in the vegetable garden in late May to June.

Courgettes like a sunny, sheltered spot and plenty of moisture so we water them regularly. Each plant produces lots of courgettes and it's easy to get overwhelmed, which is why we only have a couple of plants. There are various colours available, but I like the green ones best.

I enjoyed eating a new recipe recently with Annabel Westray, a great gardener and cook. She sliced small courgettes thinly with a potato peeler and fanned the raw slices out on a flat plate in a circular pattern like a flower. Then she poured over a mint dressing. It was so summery and delicious.

Chives are really easy to grow and have a mild, onion taste that is useful as a garnish.

Chives

Courgettes

Cucumbers

Summer

Cucumbers
There are two types of cucumber – ones to grow indoors and those for outdoors – and lots of different varieties to choose from, with some forming a little bush and others having a trailing habit.

We grow ours in an unheated greenhouse and I like short, smooth-skinned ones that are about half the length of traditional cucumbers. I'm not a fan of the prickly ones. I've tried growing from seed without success, and one year I planted them in the greenhouse too early and they wilted. I now grow two plants in the greenhouse in late May. Slugs and snails eat young plants so it's worth protecting them. We pinch out the growing tip when we see that there are seven leaves as it makes for stronger plants.

They take around 12 weeks before they are ready to harvest, and the more you pick, the more cucumbers the plant will produce. Last year, our two plants produced around 70 cucumbers – they just kept on coming! As well as eating them in salads, I like to pickle them.

Dill
One of my favourite herbs, dill is brilliant chopped and scattered over the top of fish and new potatoes. We use a lot of it. It's an attractive-looking plant in its own right, with feathery leaves and little, acid-yellow flowers.

Dill tends to bolt if it's transplanted, so we direct sow seed in shallow drills in the raised beds, first in late spring once there's no longer a risk of frost, then twice more over the course of the summer to make sure we have a continuous supply.

It likes a sunny, sheltered spot. We keep them weed free and well watered, particularly in dry spells as again they can bolt if they become stressed. Young plants are prone to greenfly, slugs, and snails so we keep an eye out for these. All being well, leaves are ready to harvest after about eight weeks after we've sown them.

French beans
Nowadays, I only grow the climbing variety of French bean as I find the dwarf ones entail too much bending over to pick them! Also the

dwarf ones only produce beans over a few weeks, but the climbing varieties produce beans from midsummer to early autumn. We plant them at the end of one of the raised beds and grow them up short bean sticks that are a good height for me to harvest.

You can either start beans off in small pots indoors from late April onwards, or direct sow in late spring to early summer when there's no longer a chance of frost. We dig over the area first, adding in well-rotted manure or our homemade compost. If we are growing climbing beans, we put the supports in first and will either use bamboo canes or hazel poles tied with gardening twine.

French beans like lots of water and warmth, so we plant a few in a sunny spot and water them regularly. I like to pick them when they are young, harvesting every day, which encourages more to come.

French tarragon
This is a perennial herb with fine leaves and a strong, aniseed-like flavour that is really good with fish dishes. I find it best to buy small plants as I've read that it's not easy to grow from seed. It likes lots of sun and shelter. To improve drainage, I always add a good handful of grit beneath the plant, whether I'm growing it in the ground or in a pot.

Being herbaceous, French tarragon dies back over winter but, as it's borderline hardy, it's worth protecting with horticultural fleece to make sure that it comes back. I grow them in pots and bring them into the greenhouse over winter. There is another form called Russian tarragon, but I don't grow that as although it's hardier, the flavour is rubbish.

Kalette
This was a new vegetable to me. They're also known as flower sprouts and are a cross between kale and Brussels sprouts, and they do look a bit like Brussels sprouts. I'm not a great fan of kale, but

I use short canes to support French beans, I find them easy to pick at this height.

Dill

French tarragon

Kalette

Cantaloupe melon

these have a milder taste. You pick them later in the season as you would sprouts.

I love to try new things and bought them as little plug plants from Sarah Raven and Thompson & Morgan, but you can also sow them from seed, which can be started off indoors in March to April or direct sown from April to early June. We put plug plants in the ground around June or July somewhere sunny.

Kalette like to have the soil nice and firm around them to stop them rocking in the wind and also benefit from being watered while they are getting established. We put in some form or support too as they grow to around 30 inches (75 centimetres) tall.

The first time we grew Kalette, they got badly attacked by cabbage white butterfly, so we threw over a fine mesh to protect them. We still ended up with a relatively good harvest from November to March.

Melons

We grow these in the greenhouse sometimes with success, other times not, as they need lots of warmth, humidity, and moisture to produce decent fruit. Anyway, it's fun to try.

There are two sorts of melon that can be grown successfully in England, and we always grow cantaloupe, rather than honeydew. They are a close relative of cucumber, and in the right conditions, produce between two to four melons per plant.

Buy them as young plants and train them up canes, tying them in with string. Throughout the growing season, we water them regularly at the base of the stem to keep the compost moist but making sure that it's not saturated. We also feed them with Tomorite, or something similar that is high in potassium. As soon as the leaves start to die back and the fruit is ripening, we reduce the watering and feeding.

Snails and slugs can be a problem, so we keep an eye out for them. Over the summer months, we make sure the greenhouse is well ventilated by opening the door early and closing it at the end of the day.

The Alitex glasshouse at the end of the vegetable garden is ideal for starting off seedlings and cuttings, growing tomatoes and cucumbers, as well as storing tender plants over the winter months.

Nasturtiums
Gosh, nasturtiums are easy to grow – you just push the seeds into the soil anytime from April to July and they are up in around two weeks, flowering all the way through to the first frosts. Deadheading encourages them to flower for longer. They like lots of sunshine and don't need much in the way of watering, but I always keep an eye out for cabbage white butterfly caterpillars, as they love eating them too.

There are a number of different varieties, some grow bushy and others climb. The orange flowers are the most commonly available, and you can also get them in cream, pinks, and reds. The flowers and leaves have a peppery taste and I like using them in salads. My favourite is called 'Empress of India', which has bright red flowers.

Onions
Reliable and always useful in the kitchen, onions are another crop that's really easy to grow. There are lots of different varieties, but because we've limited space, we only grow red onions, which are more expensive in the shops.

We grow them from sets (small, immature bulbs), which we plant directly in the soil in spring. We rake over the soil before planting, then put one little onion set every 6 inches (15 centimetres) apart. The main thing is to keep the area weed free and water if too dry.

It takes just under three months for them to mature, and we know they are ready to harvest – usually early to midsummer – when the leaves collapse and turn brown. We pull them up, dry them off, cut the leaves off, and store them somewhere dry.

Onions are another useful crop that is easy to grow, reliable, and always useful in the kitchen.

Parsley
This is another easy-to-grow plant that we harvest all through summer and into autumn. I grow flat-leaf parsley, as although it tastes very similar to curly parsley, I find the flat foliage

Nasturtium flowers add a pop of bright colour to the beds and a peppery warmth to my salads too.

Nasturtium 'Empress of India'

Red onion

Parsley (flat leaf)

more attractive. We sow straight in the ground from May. They do tend to be slow to germinate – up to six weeks – so it's worth being patient.

A tip I was given is to make a long, shallow furrow, pour a kettle of boiling water in it, sprinkle in the seed, then cover the furrow lightly with soil. Apparently, it softens the hard coating of the seed and improves germination. It works for me!

We sow parsley with other herbs in a raised bed and also have some in two large pots by the back door, which we can easily access from the kitchen. Alongside are some other pots where we have thyme, sage, French tarragon, and basil plants.

Parsley will grow in sun or part shade. They are thirsty plants, so we water them a lot and also make sure they don't get swamped by weeds. We harvest from summer into autumn, snipping the stems off at the base as this encourages it to regrow.

Raspberries
Freshly picked, homegrown raspberries are delicious just as they are and so much tastier than most of those bought in a shop. They are divided into two main groups: those that fruit in summer and ones that fruit in autumn; we grow both.

There are a number of different varieties to choose from, and when we moved to Henley, we planted yellow raspberries. They fruited well but the verdict was that everyone enjoyed the usual red raspberries, so out they went.

We used to have just the autumn-fruiting ones, which fruit on growth made earlier in the season; those that fruit in summer produce fruit on one-year-old canes. Raspberries like a sunny, sheltered spot. You can plant canes in either autumn or spring, and we soak the roots in water before putting them in the ground about 2 inches (5 centimetres) deep, spacing them around 18 to 24 inches (45 to 60 centimetres) apart, with 6 feet (1.8 metres) between the rows.

Freshly picked, homegrown raspberries are the best.

Summer

During the growing season, we water them regularly as raspberries are thirsty plants, and mulch and feed each spring. We support the canes with horizontal wires attached to posts at the end of the rows.

Pruning autumn-fruiting raspberries is really straightforward – we just cut back all the old, fruited wood to the ground in February. With summer-fruiting varieties, it's a matter of separating out the old wood that has already fruited and cutting that to the ground, then cutting out any of the weak green stems, leaving only the strongest – around six to eight per plant – and tying those into the supports. Both sorts produce suckers, so these are best removed, unless of course we want more plants, in which case we replant them.

Salad leaves

Homegrown salad leaves taste so good. There's a wide range of different flavours, colours, and textures and they are easy and quick to grow. We sow a few every couple of weeks from March to September to get a constant supply, and many of the loose-leaf ones work well as cut-and-come-again. One of our favourites is little gem lettuce, a mini cos lettuce that produces a small head packed with crunchy, green leaves around a dense heart.

We direct sow thinly at about ½ inch (1 centimetre) deep, and cover with a fine layer of soil. Once the seedlings have emerged, we thin them out to around 4–8 inches (10–20 centimetres) apart.

Lettuces get stressed and bolt if they dry out too much or get overly hot, so we keep them well watered. Slugs and snails can quickly eat their way through a whole crop, so we put grit around our plants and pick them off when we spot them. Ours inevitably bolt in the end and I try to pick them before it happens.

This year, we are growing a rocket called 'Apollo', which has larger leaves and a milder taste than the classic rocket. We are growing it in raised beds, which means that flea beetles, which make tiny holes in the leaves, are less likely to be attracted to them. The seeds were given to me by my dear friend and mentor Alan Titchmarsh, who knows a bit about veggies!

I've tried growing lamb's lettuce, which we like, but they take up too much space. I found that I could use half of one of my raised beds of lamb's lettuce in a fortnight.

Shallots
These are milder tasting than regular onions and I use them roasted, chopped, added to sauces, and caramelized. There are a number of varieties with different shapes and flavours, but we like banana shallots best of all as they are larger, easier to peel, and taste as good as the smaller ones.

We grow them from sets, which we plant in early spring, although there are some varieties that you can plant from late October. They like the same conditions as onions and do well in our raised beds.

Plant the sets with the tip just poking out. Each set produces a cluster of shallots, so space them around 8 inches (20 centimetres) apart to give them plenty of space. Keep the area free of weeds and water them only when it's been really dry. It's worth keeping an eye out for slugs and snails as they like to eat the young leaves. In mid- to late summer, when the leaves are turning yellow, it's time to harvest.

Spring onions
These are a useful little onion to have to hand. They are as easy as anything to grow and take up little space in the vegetable garden. We grow them in the raised beds, sowing seeds from March onwards in a shallow drill about ¾ inch (2 centimetres) deep.

They like to grow in a sunny spot and are usually ready to harvest after about eight weeks or so. Spring onions are great for salads and shredded into rice and pasta.

Strawberries
We were having an evening picnic on a walking holiday in France when we first tried 'Gariguette' strawberries. They tasted amazing – best strawberries ever. This was years ago, and we brought back plants from the local market. Since moving, we have

Lettuce 'Little Gem'

Shallot

Spring onion

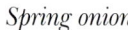
Strawberry 'Gariguette'

planted them again. It's no wonder they are one of the favourite varieties in France.

We grow them in a raised bed, but you can grow them in pots, window boxes, or even grow bags. Buy little plants in pots over the summer or as bare-root runners in spring or autumn. We put netting over them to keep the birds off and straw around them to lift the fruit off the soil. They usually ripen in June. Last year, we found that the mice enjoyed them too, so they had to be dispensed with.

During the growing season, we water the strawberries well and feed with a high-potash feed. Growing them in our raised beds means that they are at just the right height to pick. I lift the strawberries that are nearly ripe on top of a leaf so that they are in the light rather than sitting in the slight dark or damp.

Strawberries seem to fruit pretty well for three to four years but then tend to become a bit congested, so we dig them up, pull the plants apart, and replant only the healthiest, younger ones. We also put in new plants from our own runners.

Thyme

Gardener and TV presenter Adam Frost came to do a *Gardeners' World* special, and we planted up my large pot in the vegetable garden with a variegated thyme. The next year, it reverted to green but it still makes a nice, central feature and is a useful herb in the kitchen.

I grow two sorts of thyme in the garden: lemon thyme and broad-leaved thyme. They are helpful for adding different flavours to my cooking. Both types of thyme are incredibly easy to grow and, being evergreen, I think they look rather nice all year round.

Lemon thyme, as the name suggests, has lemon-scented foliage, which is bright green. It forms a compact, rounded, evergreen shrub with pink to lavender flowers, and has a slightly milder flavour compared to common thyme. It grows to around 18 inches (45 centimetres) tall.

This lovely pot of thyme is a central feature in the vegetable garden and is beautifully framed by an arch of Trachelospermum *at the entrance.*

Broad-leaved thyme has large, dark leaves that are highly scented and tiny, lilac-pink flowers. It gets to around 10 inches (25 centimetres) tall. I grow these from young plants and have found that they like full sun and, in fact, seem to be remarkably drought tolerant, so established plants in the ground don't need watering.

You can pick thyme all year round, although I've heard that it tastes best when the plants are in flower. Once flowering is over, I trim them back to keep them nice and bushy.

I grow both lemon thyme and broad-leaved thyme as they help add different flavours to cooking.

Tomatoes

We grow tomatoes in the greenhouse, and I select those with the best flavour. We like the little cherry ones, especially one Alan Titchmarsh recommended to me called 'Sungold', which produces sweet, thin-skinned, golden yellow fruit and is resistant to disease.

We have two narrow beds at each end of the greenhouse, and we clear them out every year and fill them with new compost from growbags. We put three tomato plants on each end along with a cucumber and support them on canes.

Cordon tomatoes, such as 'Sungold' and 'Gardener's Delight', produce better fruit if they have a single stem, so I simply snap off any side shoots. I remember doing this as a child in the greenhouse. My dad taught me, and it was fun to nip off the side shoots every couple of days.

We water and feed them regularly, tying them to their support canes as needed. When the main stem reaches the top of the support, we nip off the tip to stop it growing any taller. We allow the fruit to ripen on the plant and harvest as often as we can, as ripe fruits damage easily.

We grow our cordon tomatoes on a single stem, snapping off side shoots.

Q & A
Jekka McVicar VMH

I met Jekka in Bristol over 40 years ago when she was just starting out. I was doing a charity cooking demonstration, and she had a wonderful selection of her homegrown herbs for the audience to buy, beautifully arranged on a trestle table at the back of the hall. From that day, I knew that with her knowledge, enthusiasm, and flair, she would go on to do great things. Today, she is a leading expert on growing herbs.

What are your five favourite perennial culinary herbs?

Fresh herbs can quite simply transform a meal into a feast. These five are easy-to-grow perennial herbs, meaning they last more than two years.

Chives (*Allium schoenoprasum*) have delicious, onion-flavoured leaves and edible flowers that look beautiful in salads.

French tarragon (*Artemisia dracunculus*). This herb is how I met Mary more than 35 years ago, when she was giving a talk in aid of the Red Cross. It's the Rolls-Royce of anise flavours and helps with digesting rich foods.

Lemon thyme (*Thymus* 'Culinary Lemon'). This lovely, lemon-scented thyme combines well with sweet and savoury dishes and is delicious with fish.

Rosemary (*Salvia rosmarinus*) is a must-have evergreen herb. It's wonderful with roast vegetables and tomato soup or made into a tea that is said to help restore the memory.

Spearmint 'Tashkent' (*Mentha spicata* 'Tashkent') is my favourite mint and I have it growing outside my back door. It's great with strawberries, in mint sauce, or stirred into yoghurt. Grow it in a large pot to keep it from spreading around the garden.

Q & A Jekka McVicar

What are your five favourite annual culinary herbs?

Annual herbs die once they have set seed. These five are simple to grow and full of flavour.

Basil (*Ocimum basilicum*). Sow basil in late spring under cover. Always water in the morning, never at night, as he hates going to bed wet!

Coriander (*Coriandrum sativum*). Sow in early spring – or, even better, early autumn – directly into a large pot or well-prepared garden bed. You can then harvest through the winter as the plant is happy in frost down to -5°C (23°F).

Dill (*Anethum graveolens*). Sow dill in spring in a window box or large pot to ensure a good crop of leaves and a healthy harvest of seeds, which are fabulous for pickling.

Parsley (*Petroselinum crispum*). This is a biennial often grown as an annual. Without doubt, the best time to sow it is in early autumn when the soil is warm and there is plenty of moisture in the soil and air. You can harvest well into the winter and it will survive the frosts.

Mustard 'Red Frills' (*Brassica juncea* 'Red Frills'). This herb transforms salads and sandwiches, adding a lovely crunch and a peppery bite.

When should perennial herbs be divided?

I divide mint in autumn when it starts to die back. French tarragon is best divided in spring once the risk of frost has passed. Chives can be divided either in autumn or in spring, both work well.

When is the best time to prune perennial herbs?

As a general rule of thumb, prune evergreen perennial herbs such as rosemary after they've flowered. This helps stop them becoming woody and encourages fresh, compact growth. Top tip: always prune within the green, never in the old wood as it will not produce new growth.

What is your favourite tool or piece of kit for growing herbs?

I have two favourites: my beloved, ancient secateurs, which I clean and sharpen every day, and my hori hori gardening knife. It's a recent addition but is absolutely indispensable for weeding, dividing, and planting.

Autumn

Autumn is a time I find myself looking at borders and thinking about what I am going to do in the following year and how to get more colour in the garden. Fortunately, asters have been much improved, as these days, they don't suffer from rust in the way they did when I first started gardening. There's a bigger choice of things like dahlias and salvias too, which are wonderful for colour later in the season.

As well as taking stock of what's what, autumn is also the time to tidy up the garden, mulch, and cover things up in time for cold weather. I've learned my lesson with penstemons and now don't cut them back until spring, as I find tender plants such as these survive better if they are left intact over the winter months.

I do prefer spring and summer to autumn, and don't focus too much on autumn leaf colour as I'm not out in the garden quite as much. That said, it is a peaceful time of year, with less happening.

Key autumn plants

While autumn is definitely a quieter time of year, I still enjoy having plants to bring interest and colour to the garden, and find that these days there is greater choice than ever before. Here are some of my recommendations for September to November.

Anemone (Japanese anemone, windflower)

One perennial plant that I'm currently experimenting with is Japanese anemone. They are a lovely, reliable addition to the garden for late summer and early autumn, when many other plants are beginning to fade. I find Japanese anemones tend to spread everywhere, and the regular ones, which grow to about 3 to 5 feet (1 to 1.5 metres) tall, become quite dominant, but I've chosen the dwarf ones in white, as I think they're attractive and bloom for a good, long time.

I find it easier to get autumn colour in the garden now with rust-resilient asters and anemones.

I bought one called *Anemone* 'Elfin Swan', which grows to 18 to 20 inches (45 to 50 centimetres) tall and flowers from summer to autumn. Also, the Japanese anemone, *A.* x *hybrida* 'Pretty Lady Maria' reaches around 20 inches (50 centimetres) tall. These sorts of anemones spread easily and they're nice to fill gaps. If you don't want too many of them, you can thin them out in spring by digging them up and dividing them.

Anemone flowers, which appear to float above their slim, elegant, wiry stems, come in various colours, from dark and soft pinks to pure white, and can be single or double. They thrive in part shade but will tolerate a sunny spot as long as the soil remains moist. In spring, we cut back and tidy up dead leaves and stems, then over the flowering season, we deadhead lots as we do with roses.

Antirrhinum (snapdragon)

Over the years, I've had a lot of snapdragons here and they are magnificent, flowering from late summer to autumn. They last really well as a cut flower. When I pick flowers for the house, I pick just above a pair of leaves as this encourages more flowers. Some people mix them with other flowers in the vase, but I like them best on their own.

In our garden, they come back each year as they are in a sheltered position. I buy them as plug plants or you can sow them from seed, either in autumn or spring. The seeds are tiny and I haven't had great success growing them. Whichever you prefer, plants need to be protected from the cold and shouldn't be put in the ground until all danger of frost is over.

They seem to do best in full sun, somewhere relatively sheltered, and like moist, well-drained soil. They tend to spread themselves out, and during the growing season, we pinch out some of the tips to make plants bushier. They grow to about 24 inches (60 centimetres) tall.

Aster and *Symphyotrichum* (aster, Michaelmas daisy)

There are many asters that have been bred to be rust resistant and they are great plants for bridging the transition between summer

Anemone *'Elfin Swan'*
(windflower)

Antirrhinum
(snapdragon)

Aster *x* frikartii *'Mönch'*
(aster)

Callicarpa bodinieri
(Bodinier beautyberry)

and autumn. They come in a range of colours from white and pastel shades to intense shades of deep pinks and purples. They make a great cut flower and last for ages in a vase. They come in lots of different sizes, but I don't like the very squat ones, as somehow, they don't seem right. I like them a bit taller, and I generally put them at the very back of the border where I think they look great.

Asters don't tend to be fussy about soil and any average soil is fine as long as it's moist and well drained. They like sun, dappled or partial shade, and a bit of shelter. We always dig a hole slightly deeper than the pot they come in and add a bit of grit into it before putting them in place. We've found it's a good idea to allow lots of space around them to help air circulation and avoid problems with mildew.

Although we water them well while they are establishing, asters don't like sitting in a puddle of water for long periods, so we only water when the weather is particularly dry. In midsummer, we pinch out about a third of the flowering stems to encourage a longer flowering period. Depending on their height, they sometimes need a bit of support. We cut down old stems in early spring.

Aster x *frikartii* 'Mönch' is a beautiful aster with soft, green leaves and masses of large, lilac flowers that go on and on. It grows to around 24 inches (60 centimetres) tall, and we stake it, otherwise it flops over.

In autumn, I find myself looking at borders and planning how to get more colour into the garden.

Callicarpa bodinieri (Bodinier beautyberry)
This fine-looking, deciduous shrub was a gift from Lucy's brother, the gardener and designer Chris Young. It's a beauty, with clusters of pretty purple-blue berries against bare stems in autumn and leaves that turn from dark green to golden red before falling. The berry-laden branches look wonderful in a jug just by themselves.

It prefers neutral to slightly acidic soil that is fertile, moist, and free draining in either full sun or partial shade. It's best to prune for size and shape and to encourage bushier plants in late winter to early spring, before the new growth starts to appear. It reaches a maximum height of around 8 feet (2.5 metres). I found that I had to keep it well watered in the hot summer of 2025 as it suffered in the heat. I also gave it a deep mulch, as I'd hate it to die!

Dahlia
These perennials give colour and interest later in the season and look lovely in the garden, flowering from summer all the way through to the first frosts. They also make excellent cut flowers.

We buy them as tubers as this is the fastest and most reliable way to grow them. They come in all sorts of colours, shapes, and sizes, and each year, I like trying all different ones, which I mostly buy from Sarah Raven, who has an extensive collection. I haven't got a big picking bed at this house, so I put a few at the back of the borders that I can cut for the house.

We tend to start tubers off sometime in early spring in the greenhouse, putting them in pots of multipurpose compost. We give them an initial watering but then leave them alone until they start to shoot – usually after two to three weeks – then we water them sparingly as dahlias have a tendency to rot if they sit for too long in soggy soil.

Once the young plants have three pairs of leaves, I take out the tip of the main shoot along with the first pair of leaves. Later on, once plants have really got going, Sarah Raven recommends taking out all but five shoots (so the plant grows with just five stems), as apparently this results in stronger plants and more flowers.

We plant them out in their final position in the borders when there is no longer a chance of frost. They are best in a sunny, sheltered spot with fertile, well-drained soil. In the past, we had a few problems with slugs and snails, which love eating them, but not now as I put a mass of gravel around the plants along with a few slug pellets hidden away in it. We have a gravel drive so I just take some from the side. Grit is even better but I would have to buy it!

Once they are in the ground, we put in a sturdy wooden stake alongside the plant, and as they grow quickly, we tie in new growth

to the support every few weeks. Dahlias are renowned for being thirsty plants and like to have their roots kept relatively moist, so we give them a really good, deep watering in dry weather.

When they're in bloom and the head is past its best, I chop it off when I'm walking by – I'm very lazy and just let it drop on the ground and call it my mulch. If you do this then more flowers come.

Overall, I find dahlias are straightforward to grow and pretty trouble free. Although they are tender, we do leave some in the ground with a pile of mulch on top to protect them. With any particularly precious ones, we carefully dig them out and store them under cover in bulb fibre. These we plant out the following spring once all danger of frost has passed.

Personally, I also like the cactus ones but am not keen on the pom-poms or the ones with huge heads, which are too over the top for me. As for my favourite dahlias, I rather like the reddish black *Dahlia* 'Rip City', the blush-pink 'Silver Years', and the simple pink flowers of *D. merckii* .

Echinacea (coneflower)

I've recently started growng echinacea and they are really good news for me. Previously, I really didn't like them because they tended to have drooping petals. Now there are lots of varieties that open out like an upward-facing daisy. I really like the red ones such as 'Fatal Attraction', 'SunSeekers Red', and 'SunSeekers Pomegranate'.

Gazania (gazania, treasure flower)

These are wonderful, low-growing plants, perfect for the front of the border. Their vibrant, daisy-like flowers bring a splash of colour to the garden from May well into autumn. They have lush, green leaves that enhance the flowers, which you mostly find in orange, but I like the pink best.

I love the deep red petals of Dahlia *'Rip City' –*
it's one of my absolute favourites.

We buy plug plants and have found that they like to grow in a hot, sunny spot. Without sun, their flowers tend to close up, so we try to place them in as sunny a spot as possible. I deadhead them regularly so that we get the maximum number of flowers, and although they are remarkably drought tolerant, I do tend to water them if we have prolonged dry spells. They reach a height of about 10 to 20 inches (25 to 50 centimetres).

Magnolia grandiflora 'Exmouth' (evergreen magnolia)
This rather sumptuous, evergreen magnolia grows like lightning for us here and I'm quite proud of it. The leaves are large, glossy, and oblong with interesting brown felting underneath. It has huge, creamy white flowers in late summer and early autumn that smell wonderful.

It doesn't seem fussy about soil and both of ours are in part shade. They do like to be sheltered from strong winds. I've had this plant in Watercroft and Henley, and to stop it growing into a small tree and remain more shrub-like, we cut it back hard, but it always comes back. I water it during dry spells and feed it. Although it's not technically a climbing plant, it's first rate when trained against a wall, or you can grow it free standing, giving it plenty of space.

Nerine bowdenii (Bowden lily)
These are lovely and provide a lovely splash of colour in autumn when there's not so much of interest in the garden. Many are tender but *Nerine bowdenii* is relatively hardy in the right spot. We have found they do best with a wall behind them, as it retains extra heat. We grow them from bulbs, which we plant in spring, and they like a free-draining, poor soil in a warm, protected spot that receives a lot of sunshine.

The leaves are strappy and the flowers, which are held on strong, upright stems, come in shades of pink, red, and white. As well as looking wonderful in the garden, they work well as a long-lasting cut flower. They grow to about 18 inches (45 centimetres) tall.

Echinacea *Fatal Attraction*
(coneflower)

Gazania
(gazania, treasure flower)

Magnolia grandiflora *Exmouth*
(evergreen magnolia)

Nerine bowdenii
(Bowden lily)

Autumn

Romneya coulteri (Californian tree poppy)
I carefully dug up some of our Californian tree poppies in the autumn at Watercroft and put them into plastic pots before we put the house on the market. They are still doing very well and I absolutely love them.

    A herbaceous perennial, it flowers from July through to October. Fat buds unfurl to reveal huge, pure white flowers, which resemble crumpled tissue paper, with a deep yellow centre. The branching stems carry lots of glaucous grey leaves.

    It likes rich, well-drained soil in a sunny, sheltered spot. It's easy to fall in love with although it might not love you, but it's so wonderful that it's well worth a try.

    It's renowned for being slow to get going and doesn't respond well to disturbance. Established plants tend to have a suckering habit, and new shoots can appear at a fair distance from the original plant, so it's worth taking care where you site it. Once they got going here, they were very successful and quite exotic looking. They can grow to about 6½ feet (2 metres) high.

Although California tree poppies can be tricky to establish,
I think their huge, white flowers make them well worth the effort.

Winter

Winter is a time in the garden when we really appreciate its structural elements, such as the clipped yew hedges and urns, as there are few flowers to draw our attention. Our hedging is growing up well now and we have spiral topiary in pots.

Winter-flowering shrubs are good too and many of them are wonderfully scented. We also have snowdrops, hellebores, and little *Iris unguicularis*, which I love bringing into the house.

Before the first frost arrives, there are plenty of things to pick, including nerines, dahlias, crimson flag lilies, and penstemons (although penstemons don't last long in water). We also bring the three Christmas trees indoors, which we keep in pots, to decorate them. In late winter, when it's very chilly, I'll sit in the house looking out at the snowdrops and anticipate the primroses appearing. They are such a joy.

Overall, nothing much changes in the garden at this time of year. Invariably, I find myself thinking about what went wrong in the previous season and making notes of changes we can make to improve things.

Key winter plants

I have to admit that during the winter months, I spend little time out in the garden, but I love looking out of the kitchen window and seeing things coming up. I always love bringing flowers indoors to make displays, and winter is no exception. Here are some plants that I find invaluable from November to February.

Acacia pravissima (Oven's wattle, mimosa)
Our old mimosa was done in by frost, and when we were thinking of replacing it, I remembered this one that I'd rather liked at a friends' garden down at Lymington, Hampshire. It has a weeping

The seedheads of honesty catch the winter light. They self-seed each year.

habit, and although it has small, fragrant, fluffy, yellow flowers in spring like a regular mimosa, the leaves are quite different. Instead of being feathery, they are small and triangular, running the length of the slim, pendent branches.

It came from a specialist nursery called Pan Global Plants in Gloucestershire, and apparently, it's one of the hardiest there is. Even if it does get caught out by frost, it will often reshoot from the base, and it's very fast growing initially. The nursery recommended it does best in a sunny, sheltered spot.

It likes neutral to acid soil that is well drained. It will grow quite vigorously into a large, evergreen shrub or small tree to 16 feet (5 metres) tall. So far it is doing well.

Cornus mas (cornelian cherry)
Cornelian cherry is a reliable, deciduous shrub or small tree that produces lots of little, bright yellow, highly scented flowers in late winter to very early spring, often on bare branches before the leaves appear. The flowers are followed by oblong, red fruits that are edible but are quite tart and not worth bothering with. I've heard that some people use them to make jams and syrups, although I've not tried it.

In autumn, the oval, green leaves turn a striking reddish purple. It's not particularly fussy about soil type so is quite adaptable, but overall, does best in well-drained, fertile soil. It prefers full sun to partial shade, although the more sunshine it gets, the better its fruit production.

We watered it while it was getting going, but once established, it is remarkably tolerant of drought. It is extremely hardy. We prune in late winter to maintain shape and take off dead wood. I pick it for the house when the yellow flowers appear. It's not as profuse as forsythia and grows to 16 feet (5 metres) tall, though we prune ours shorter.

Cyclamen
We have both the autumn-flowering (*Cyclamen hederifolium*) and the winter- to spring-flowering cyclamen (*C. coum*) in the garden. If cyclamen is happy, it tends to self-seed around, and we're hoping we'll end up with great drifts of them.

Acacia pravissima
(Oven's wattle)

Cornus mas
(cornelian cherry)

Cyclamen hederifolium
(ivy-leaved cyclamen)

Daphne odora *'Aureomarginata'*
(gold-edged winter daphne)

C. hederifolium is a hardy little cyclamen that flowers slightly earlier than *C. coum*, producing dainty, reflexed flowers in October to November. It also comes in various shades of pinks. The dark green leaves are distinctive, looking more like those of ivy, and often have pretty silver patterning. It likes the same humus-rich, shady conditions as *C. coum* and the tubers are planted in exactly the same way. I find it best to buy in it flower rather than dry tubers. They grow to 4¾ inches (12 centimetres).

C. coum is another hardy, pretty little cyclamen that, for my mind, is well worth having in the garden. It flowers in late winter to early spring with delicate reflexed petals that come in white as well as shades of pink and magenta. The dark green leaves are rounded or kidney-shaped and often have silver or grey-green markings. They grow to 4 inches (10 centimetres).

They do best in humus-rich soil somewhere partially shaded. We've planted them beneath our trees, where the light can reach them in winter, but they are protected from the sun during summer. They also look great beneath shrubs and naturalized in grass. Originally, I bought them in pots while they were in flower, initially as an experiment, but we've had reliable results.

I read that you shouldn't plant the two types of cyclamen together as the *C. hederifolium* tends to take over, but we have and they seem fine so far.

I love having their pretty little flowers just by themselves in a small vase. I pick them by giving the stem a gentle tug so that I get a long tail that I then cut to the length suitable for the vase. They last for about five days and look so attractive. They are worth considering when there's not much else in flower.

Daphne

These winter-flowering shrubs are lovely and are particularly welcome when there is so little else flowering in the garden. We've got two different sorts, and the scent is so wonderful. They are good for cutting, and the flowers smell even more intense and sweet when they are indoors in the warmth.

Daphne bholua 'Mary Rose' is an evergreen shrub with narrow, glossy, dark green leaves throughout the year, and from mid-winter to early spring, it produces clusters of deep purple-pink buds that open to relatively large flowers. These are pale in the centre and deep pink at the edges and have a powerful, sweet smell. I've just been given one by my lovely neighbours, Anne and Penny, and am taking great care of it. It grows to about 5 to 8 feet (1.5 to 2.5 metres).

D. odora 'Aureomarginata' is a compact daphne with dark green leaves edged in golden yellow, and purply-pink buds open out to pretty clusters of pale pink flowers in late winter to early spring. Again, the flowers have an exceptionally strong, sweet smell. It grows to about 5 feet (1.5 metres).

It's worth watering them in dry periods but they hate to be waterlogged, and we give them a good mulch in spring using well-rotted manure. Daphnes do best in dappled shade, with a light, free-draining soil. They can be tricky to get going and hate being transplanted, but we've found that once they are established, they flower beautifully.

We don't do much in the way of pruning as it's not necessary, but we do prune them lightly to improve the shape and take out any damaged stems, and I do like cutting off a little stem to bring indoors.

Forsythia

I find this is an excellent shrub. It's easy to grow, fully hardy, and deciduous, and I love picking lots of the twiggy stems of bright yellow flowers for the house. It has a relatively short period of interest, which is why I planted it in the bed at the back of the tennis court where it's out of the way and I can cut as much as I like. The cheerful, bell-shaped flowers appear on bare, arching stems early in the year, when there's little else to pick. The green leaves appear after flowering.

In our garden, I start picking stems in late February. I find the best time to pick them is just as the buds are coming into flower. I put the stems in a pot of water in the garage, then when the flowers start opening up, I bring them into the house. I often have a huge jug of it and it's such a lovely bright colour and looks amazing just on its own. Once it's over, I just replace it with another.

I've learned from experience that it's best to buy forsythia when it's in bloom, and I like to choose one with flowers that are not *too* bright, although I'm not sure of the name of the variety. I always look for a nice shape as it's difficult to change that.

It's tough, fast growing, and not terribly fussy about where it is sited. Although it tolerates shade, it will bloom best in full sun. Pruning is key to promoting flowers and we cut the stems right back in late spring. I look for the branches that have finished flowering and cut three to four buds up from the base of the plant. All the new stems that develop over the rest of the year will bear flowers the following spring, so always prune straight after flowering. It can grow to 10 feet (3 metres) high.

Galanthus (snowdrop)

I love snowdrops. They are some of the earliest plants to flower in the garden and they are so lovely to pick. I like to have maybe six or eight in a tiny vase and they look wonderful. Although there are lots of different snowdrops available these days, I tend to simply choose those that have broad leaves and are particularly tall. I have them in various parts of the garden, and when I look out of the kitchen window, I can just see some of them growing around a tree near the entrance to the vegetable garden.

It's best to plant snowdrops in early spring in the green – just after flowering and while they still have leaves. You can also plant dry bulbs, which are cheaper, in autumn, but it's often less successful.

Snowdrops like partial shade in soil that is moist, well drained, and rich in humus. They need very little attention, although deadheading them can help the bulbs conserve their energy for the following year, and if they start to become congested, then we dig them up and divide them. The great joy is that they spread with time.

Galanthus elwesii is known as the giant or greater snowdrop, and this lovely variety is relatively tall and one of the earliest to flower. It has large, single, white, nodding bells with little green spots on

Forsythia

A bright splash of colour when not much else is in flower, forsythia cheers up dull winter days.

Snowdrops are the earliest plants to flower in my garden, and I love to look out of the window and see their white bells under the tree.

Galanthus elwesii
(giant or greater snowdrop)

the inner side of the petals and broad, grey-green leaves. It reaches 8¼ inches (22 centimetres) tall, towering above other snowdrops, and it has distinctive leaves that fold neatly inside one another.

G. elwesii 'Grumpy' is another early flowerer, blooming in late winter to early spring. It's bigger than most snowdrops and grows to about 6 inches (15 centimetres) tall, so it's easier to spot in the distance. It has large, single, pure white flowers with an inner segment marked with two green spots above an upside-down V shape that looks a bit like a grumpy face. The glaucous, green leaves are also relatively broader. When I pick them, I put them under the cold tap to prolong flowering.

Hamamelis x *intermedia* 'Pallida' (witch hazel)
This witch hazel shrub or small tree is a joy in winter, producing masses of sweetly scented, sulphur-yellow, spidery flowers on bare branches from around December to February. It's one of my favourite witch hazels and looks particularly lovely alongside daffodils. Although witch hazels come in orangey colours too, I think that the yellow 'Pallida' is the best. It is stunning in late winter.

As well as being a beauty in winter, in autumn, its bright green leaves turn lovely shades of orange, red, and yellow. It likes to grow in full sun or partial shade, somewhere protected from cold winds in moist, well-drained soil, ideally an acidic to neutral soil. We mulch around the base each year and keep plants watered during dry spells, especially while they are becoming established.

Hamamelis don't need much in the way of pruning, but, if need be, we simply remove any dead, damaged, and congested stems once flowering is over. It reaches a height of 10 feet (3 metres).

Witch hazels are really expensive shrubs. I only have one and gulped at the price. I made sure to choose one that has a very good shape, and I positioned it in the garden where we can really appreciate it. It's far too good to put it at the end of the garden where you have to make an effort to go and enjoy it.

Witch hazel really brightens up the garden in the middle of winter.

Helleborus (hellebore)
I invariably have hellebores in my winter pots near the front door. Once they are over, I keep them in the hosta bed. I particularly like white hellebores or Christmas rose (*Helleborus niger*), as white goes with everything. It reaches about 12 inches (30 centimetres) tall. I've also got some coloured ones, which I leave in a pot and tuck behind the greenhouse once they've finished flowering. I simply water from time to time, and they come back into flower beautifully around February time.

I also like 'Angel Glow', which is a compact, evergreen hellebore that flowers from late winter to early spring, producing lots of pale pink flowers that fade to light green as they age. The leathery leaves in a blue-green colour are attractive too. We find deadheading helps encourage the plant to put on new growth for the following year, and it grows to 16 inches (40 centimetres) high.

Hellebores are really easy to grow and flower reliably early in the year. Often, the foliage is good too. Hellebores are happy in either sun or partial shade. When growing them in pots, we use a loam-based compost. Once plants are established, they are relatively tolerant of drought, but we water them in particularly dry spells and mulch them every year to retain moisture. To keep them looking smart, we cut back the old leaves once the new foliage and flowers start to appear.

When picking them for the house, I float the flower heads with some of the leaves in a large, shallow glass bowl. It looks great in the centre of a low table so that you can see over them. They flop if they are cut when in full bloom. I have been told to blanch the stalk ends in boiling water, but it didn't work for me. If you leave the flowers until they are going to seed and pick them then, they last well in a vase.

Iris unguicularis 'Mary Barnard' (Algerian iris)
Sometimes referred to as the Algerian or winter iris, this lovely, robust little iris has delicately scented, intense purple-blue flowers and dark, evergreen, grass-like leaves. It flowers from mid-winter through to spring, and I have masses of them behind

When picking hellebores for the house, I choose a large, shallow glass bowl and float the flower heads in it along with some of the leaves.

Helleborus
(hellebore)

Iris unguicularis
'Mary Barnard' (Algerian iris)

Jasminum nudiflorum
(winter jasmine)

the nerines at the base of a south-facing wall, as they like well-drained soil in a sheltered sunny spot. They grow to 16 inches (40 centimetres) high. Sometimes the frost catches them but as the weather improves more flowers come.

I like to pick the slim buds every day as they appear – getting them before the little blue tits take them – and bring them into the house to open out. If any are left on the plant, I deadhead frantically to get more blooms. Friends are often surprised to see these little treasures in a small jug on the kitchen table.

When we moved to Henley-on-Thames, I met Penny Godfrey, a kindred spirit and a passionate gardener. I divided some of my 'Mary Barnard' irises as a gift to Penny. Like me, she gets excited when the beautiful dark blue gems of iris appear amidst the tall leaves, intermittently from early winter through to spring, even on the coldest of days. When we moved, Penny also introduced me to Hambledon Gardening Club. We share many gardening lectures and garden visits together.

Jasminum nudiflorum (winter jasmine)

Winter jasmine is a lovely, deciduous shrub that has long, arching, bright green stems and small leaves. It can be left to ramble along a wall or tied in on some form of support so that it climbs vertically. In winter, it produces lots of tiny, fragrant, bright yellow flowers, often before the leaves appear. It works really well as a cut flower, and I'll often bring a few stems of it into the house, which is a joy when there's little else in bloom.

We have it in a sheltered, sunny spot. It's quite vigorous – it can grow to 10 feet (3 metres) high – so we prune it regularly to keep it neat. I always buy plants when they are in flower as I like the slightly paler ones and always look for one with a good shape.

Laurus nobilis (bay tree)

We have three bay trees in big terracotta pots on the terrace behind the house. We keep them clipped into neat lollipop shapes, and their dark, evergreen leaves provide good formal structure all year round. For the summer months, we underplant them with *Erigeron karvinskianus* (Mexican fleabane), and the little daisy flowers spill nicely over the edge and bloom for ages.

When we originally planted the bay trees, we used a soil-based compost and positioned the pots in full sun. Garden designer Bunny Guinness recommended cutting the base of the pots so that the roots can go down into the soil, which we've done and works really well.

During the summer, we keep them regularly watered and clip the foliage so that it becomes nice and dense. I'll often use the aromatic leaves in cooking and it's fine to snip a couple off at any time of year. In early summer, some of the leaves can turn yellow, so I just pick them off. Bay trees are renowned for being slow growing, but they can eventually reach 26 feet (8 metres) tall.

We have found that young bay trees are slightly tender and can be affected by severe cold and frost, so we keep them somewhere nice and sheltered. In the previous house, when we first had them, we always covered them with netting or fleece over the winter. It didn't look very nice but it did stop them from becoming damaged.

Lonicera fragrantissima (winter-flowering honeysuckle)

This winter-flowering, shrubby honeysuckle is a joy in late winter and early spring. It has sweetly scented, creamy white flowers, often on branches that are almost leafless. It's deciduous, although a few leaves often remain on the branches, and the new, oval, green leaves, flushed in purple, appear in spring.

It grows best in full sun, preferably somewhere a bit protected from wind so that the buds don't get damaged. We water well in dry spells while it's getting itself established.

It needs very little in the way of maintenance: we just give it a light pruning after flowering, taking out the older stems to maintain a good shape and make space for the new. It is great for picking to add to a vase and it smells beautiful. All of the winter-scented flowers are worth having near a doorway or path where they can be appreciated daily.

I love our neatly clipped lollipops of bay in their pots bringing interest to the patio area, alongside the pruned rose beds. We prune the roses in October or November – the hardest prune takes place in March.

Lonicera fragrantissima
(winter-flowering honeysuckle)

Sarcococca confusa
(sweet box)

Viburnum *x* bodnantense
'Dawn' (arrowwood)

All the winter-scented flowers are worth having in a spot near the house, where they can be appreciated daily.

Sarcococca confusa (sweet box)

Sweet box is a dense, evergreen shrub with glossy, dark green, oval leaves and highly scented, tiny, creamy white flowers along the stems in winter. There are a number of different varieties, but we like *Sarcococca confusa* best. It has a strong fragrance and grows up to 5 feet (1.5 metres) tall.

I often use sarcococcas in my winter pots by the front door, as it's lovely to have scented things where you pass by frequently. I put one plant in each very large plant pot and then arrange some early, large-flowered Christmas rose (*Helleborus niger*) and little variegated ivy around the edge.

In the spring, I take out all these, putting the hellebores in the hosta bed, and repot the two sarcococcas, giving them a shapely trim at the same time. If planting them in the ground, they seem to do best in moist soil, and while they are fine in sun, they are very tolerant of shade, even full shade, which makes them useful plants for certain parts of the garden where nothing much else will survive.

Viburnum x *bodnantense* 'Dawn' (arrowwood)

I always used to grow this lovely shrub as it's one of the few that flowers right through the winter, but so far, I haven't put it in this garden. It has lots of dense clusters of pretty, pale pink and white, highly scented flowers from late autumn to early spring on bare stems. The deciduous foliage is tinged bronze when it first appears, then changes to green and finally reddish purple in autumn.

It does fine in full sun or partial shade. It is drought tolerant once it's got itself established, but we always thought it best to water it for the first couple of years. The best time to prune is after flowering, which we did lightly, just enough to maintain a nice shape as well as taking the opportunity to tidy up any dead stems.

It does tend to catch the frost easily, so we always tried to position it in a warm, sheltered spot. If not, just when you think you're going to have a few twigs for the house, it seems to get caught by frost. It grows to 8 to 10 feet (2.5 to 3 metres) tall.

Winter containers

For winter, I like planting up two big terracotta pots to display either side of the front door. I use sarcococcas (sweet box) and keep the plants from one year to the next, tucking them away outdoors in a pot in the shade at the back of the greenhouse when the winter display is over. To these, I add some white hellebores, evergreen ferns, and a few deep blue pansies. I started off with white pansies but now prefer the blue. My aim is that hopefully it all looks quite cheerful and attractive.

When I'm putting together the winter pots, I like including plants that you can use in the pot and later plant in the garden. Hellebores work well in this regard. That said, I've had one of my hellebores in a pot by itself for four years. I do nothing with it apart from chucking a bucket of water over it from time to time and giving it a bit of feed in late summer. After it's flowered, I keep it behind the greenhouse and it comes up again each year. Now it's so huge that I'll never get it out of its pot.

Pansies are also very good for winter pots. Everybody's got their thoughts of what sort of pansies they like, but I keep to one or two colours, maybe cream or cream and blue. They look good and are not expensive, but it is important to deadhead constantly to keep them flowering well. If you put pansies in good soil, keep them watered, and deadhead regularly, they'll grow beautifully. I have learned not to plant them in the pots too early when it's cold and frosty.

I've always done mixed plantings and experimented with all sorts. I recently bought two white wallflowers to add to my winter pots at the front door, and they are doing brilliantly.

Inspiration for planting containers

You can find inspiration in gardening magazines and in other people's gardens. Obviously the RHS gardens, such as Wisley, are a great inspiration too. I'll often take a picture and the measurements of my pot along to a garden centre – best when it's not a busy time – and there's invariably someone who will help advise you.

That's exactly what I did when I went down to Wisley. I was just filling my two pots here for the winter and always do them the same, and I thought I'd be a bit different. I always put hellebores in them and bulbs underneath, but it was suggested that sarcococca would be good, so I started to do that.

Next winter, I plan to add in a little bit of variegated ivy around the side as I like the way it trails down. I think along with the hellebores and sweet box, it will look quite nice.

Christmas trees

We have a tradition of keeping our small, rooted Christmas trees from one year to the next. For the most part of the year, we keep them next to the greenhouse, where I am reminded to keep an eye on them and water as need be.

We grow them in large pots and it's important to feed and repot them each year. As long as you do that, you can bring them back indoors each December to decorate the house over the festive period. It's also very important to keep them watered when they are in the house over Christmas.

Garden birds

I simply love watching the birds in the garden and always feed them in winter, making sure to put feeders near the kitchen window so that we can watch them. I have one little bird feeder that attaches to the window overlooking the back garden so that we can see them up close. I also have a big cage that I put half coconuts filled with fat in that seems to be squirrel proof.

Someone once advised me to make my own coconut feeders by filling the shell with beef fat mixed with seeds, so I did just that and put it on the bird table. But in the summer heat, the beef fat just dripped out and made a mess. Really, I should have used suet, which has got a higher melting point.

At one point, we did have trouble with the bird seed dropping to the ground and attracting rats, but using the filled coconuts has helped stop this problem.

We keep our small Christmas trees from one year to the next, bringing them in over the Christmas period to decorate the house.

Bringing flowers indoors

Sometimes, in winter and spring when I'm stuck for bringing garden flowers indoors, I buy snowdrops or daffodils in tiny pots from the supermarket, or I might dig up some of my own and then position them back after flowering. I put them in a nice-looking container and top with some moss that I've also scooped up from the garden. You can usually find a bit of moss somewhere in the garden, and it really makes all the difference to the appearance.

As soon as they finish flowering, I just put everything back into the garden again and water them. After all, we're always told to plant snowdrops in the green, so it works really well.

Mulching with homemade compost, well-rotted manure, and leaf mould enriches the soil, helps suppress weeds, and improves moisture retention. It looks smart too.

Winter to-do list

Our gardener, Kevin, works in the garden throughout the year, and he likes to make sure there are enough jobs for a day a week in winter and that he's always busy.

Winter is the time to collect fallen leaves, run the mower over them to chop them up a bit, and pile them up in a cage made of wire netting to make leaf mould. We also add some to the regular compost heap. Mulching with homemade compost, well-rotted manure, and leaf mould enriches the soil, helps suppress weeds, and improves moisture retention. It looks smart too.

It's also the time to bring in garden furniture and see what needs mending or painting. We check what plants we need to cover up to protect from frost, and if we need a new compost bin, we'll make one out of old wooden pallets.

We always take the opportunity to clean our paths in winter, and if you've stone or paving, it's good to go over them with a pressure hose to clean off any moss and dirt and stop them from becoming slippery. I always keep a sack of rock salt to hand and sprinkle it on paths to stop them being slippery in icy weather. A pressure hose is good for cleaning furniture too.

Protecting the lawn
We often find squirrels dig holes in the lawn to bury chestnuts and hazelnuts, and because we don't mow over winter, we put netting over the top and stake it in place, and this does help stop them a bit. A sprinkling of chilli powder or flakes also helps to deter them further. It seems that once they've made one hole they come back and make more, so the sooner you stop them, the better. We love to play croquet, so when we want to play a game, we simply lift up the netting and then replace it when we're done.

Q & A
Tom Stuart-Smith OBE

I greatly admire Tom for his private garden, Serge Hill, in Hertfordshire, where he is experimenting with drought-tolerant, sun-loving, Mediterranean plants that he never waters. I love the fact that he enjoys weeding, and so do I.

It's so satisfying to get weeds out, roots and all. He spoils his gardeners with proper coffee at breakfast and looks after them too.

What are your recommendations for 10 of the best high-performing, drought-tolerant plants?

Amsonia hubrichtii (Arkansas bluestar), a feathery amsonia from Arkansas, in the United States.

Aster divaricatus, also known as *Eurybia divaricata* (white wood aster), is the ultimate ground cover for dry shade.

Cistus x *argenteus* **'Blushing Peggy Sammons'**, a wonderful, vivid cistus with shocking pink flowers.

Euphorbia characias subsp. *wulfenii* (Mediterranean spurge) is very well known and is indispensable.

Ferula communis (giant fennel), a good one if you like your plants huge.

Iris pallida and other bearded iris.

Laserpitium siler (laserwort) is a lovely umbel from dry slopes in southern Europe.

Lavandula (most lavender species).

Phlomis (Jerusalem sage) in many forms. I particularly value a fine-leaved form of *P. purpurea* subsp. *almeriensis*.

Salvia candelabrum (candelabrum sage), not fully hardy and needing the sharpest of drainage, but a thing of airy beauty.

Seseli hippomarathrum, a lovely, low, feathery umbel lasting months in beauty and very poorly known.

Could you suggest five tips on how to design a garden from scratch?

The most important thing to decide on is who you are and what sort of garden will suit you and your way of living. Don't be pushed about by a fancy designer with their ideas of how they would like you to live. Do you like formality or wildness, do you prefer modernity or nostalgia?

Plant trees very early on and as many as you possibly can. Most of them should be native, but do hedge your bets with a proportion of drought-tolerant exotics.

If it's an established landscape or garden you are working on, spend a bit of time looking at it and deciding what it is about the place that you value and might accentuate.

Be realistic about how much gardening needs to be done and who is going to do it. Employ a well-trained gardener if you need to and be nice to them! It will pay dividends for all.

Decide how you are going to deal with slopes. In an informal garden, this may not be so much of an issue, but in a formal garden, slopes are more of a challenge and you need to have a clear design strategy.

What are the best hedging plants for light, dry soil?

There are so many options: yew (*Taxus*), hornbeam (*Carpinus*), and myrtle (*Myrtus*) – in warm climates, both the ordinary myrtle and 'Tarentina' – are immensely smart for a low hedge.

What are your top five dahlias?

Dahlia imperialis, D. excelsa, D. merckii – all species dahlias. I generally prefer things closer to the native, although in dahlias, roses, delphiniums, and a few other plants, I ignore that completely. 'Soulman' and 'Dark Desire' are two dark red dahlias I love. I'm not a 'Café au Lait' kind of guy.

What is your favourite gardening tool or piece of kit?

A small hand fork. I love weeding, and sort of think that if you don't love weeding, you are missing one of the great joys of gardening, although that seems a very odd thing to say to many would-be gardeners.

Index

Page numbers in *italics* refer to illustrations

A
Abbott and Holder 16
Acacia pravissima 240, 242, *243*
acid soils 69
Aconitum 82, *134*, 135
Adiantum venustum 130
African lily *134*, 136
Agapanthus 134, 136, 140, 161
al fresco eating *50*, 93, 132, 135
Alchemilla mollis 73, 82, 136, *137*
Algerian iris 82, *83*, 250, *251*, 252
alkaline soils 69
Alstroemeria 35, 37, 75, 86, 136–40, *138*
amaryllis *116*, 117
Amelanchier lamarckii 69
Ammi majus 104–05, 140, *141*
Amsonia hubrichtii 264
Anchusa azurea 'Loddon Royalist' 140, *141*
Anemone 228–30, *229*
  A. 'Elfin Swan' 230, *231*
  A. × *hybrida* 'Pretty Lady Maria' 230
Antirrhinum 230, *231*
  A. tortuosum 83, 86
Argentinian vervain 175, *176*, 177
Argyranthemum 141, 142
arrowwood *256*, 257
asparagus 199–201, *200*
Aspidistra elatior 'Variegata' 130
Aster 24, 228, *229*, 230, 232
  A. divaricatus 264
  A. × *frikartii* 'Mönch' 86, 231, 232
Astrantia 141, 142
Austin, Claire 148, 168
Austin, David 68–69, 192
autumn 228–39

B
Balkan clary 86, 172, 174
Balkan spurge 105
Barlow, Mr 19
basil *198*, 201–02, *203*, 227
bay 78, 129, 252–53, *254–55*
beans, French 207–08, *209*
Beaucarnea recurvata 130
beetroot 93, 202, *203*
Berry, Alleyne 16, *17*, 18, 19, 20, 21, 24
Berry, Grandpa 14, 15
Berry, Margaret 14, 16, 18, 19, 20, 21, 61
bindweed 75
birds 52, 259
bishop's flower 104–05, 140, *141*
blackberries 15
Blackburn, Miss 18
Blackmore & Langdon 37, 144, 145
Bledlow Manor House 199
Block, Mum 24–25, 192
Block, Penny 24, 25, 41, 43, 192
Bodinier beautyberry 231, 232–33
Bolton, James 44, 62
Border Lines 62
Bougainvillea 106, *107*
Bowden lily 236, *237*
box *36*, 46, 55, 87, 91, 92, 131
Brazilian jasmine *162*, 163
Brunnera macrophylla 'Jack Frost' 154
Bryan, Felicity 29
bugloss 140, *141*
bulbs 82, 103, 105, 129
Buxus 46, 87, 131

C
Californian tree poppy *238*, 239
Callicarpa bodinieri 231, 232–33
Camellia japonica 69, 82, *83*
Cape leadwort 169
Carrington, Lord 199
carrots 199, *203*, 204
catmint 32, 46, 79, 160, *162*, 163–64
celeriac *203*, 204–05
Cerinthe 105
Chaenomeles japonica 73–74, 82, 106, *108*
Charlcombe Church 16, 22
Charlcombe Farm 21
Charles, Prince 37
cherry 169, *173*
chives 197, 205, *206*, 226, 227
Christmas rose 61, *83*, 86, 250, 257
Christmas trees 32, 259, *260–61*
cider gum 82, 111–12, *113*
Cistus × *argenteus* 'Blushing Peggy Sammons' 264
  C. × *limon 108*, 109
Clematis 'Hagley Hybrid' 32–33, 86, 142–44, *143*
climbers 86
coneflower 86, 235, *237*
containers 47, 95, 126–29, 189, 193–96, *258–59*
Convallaria majalis 108, 109
  C. m. 'Vic Pawlowski's Gold' 109, 130
coral bells *150*, 151
coriander 227
cornelian cherry 98, 242, *243*
Cornus mas 98, 242, *243*
Cosmos bipinnatus (cosmea) 86, 104, 144, *146*
courgettes 205, *206*
cranesbill 147–48, *149*
crimson flag lilies 34, 240
Crocus 61, 99, 105, *108*, 110
cucumbers 93, *206*, 207
Cyclamen 242, 244
C. coum 82, 114, 154, 242, 244
C. hederifolium 82, 130, 154, 242, *243*, 244

D
daffodils 71, 123, 262
  'Bridal Crown' 82, 120
  'February Gold' 82, 98, 120
  'Hawera' 82, 120
  'Polar Hunter' 105
  'Rijnveld's Early Sensation' 82, 98, 120
  'Silver Chimes' 37, 82, 120, *121*
  'Tête-à-tête' 82, 98, 123
  'Toto' 82, 123
Dahlia 35, 228, 233–35, 240, 265
  D. 'Labyrinth' 104
  D. merckii 82, 235
  D. 'Rip City' 82, *234*, 235
  D. 'Silver Years' 82, 235
  D. 'Sissinghurst' 104, 105
  D. 'Tom's Choice' 105
Danesfield Nursery 63, 128
Daphne 244–45
  D. bholua 'Mary Rose' 245
  D. odora 'Aureomarginata' 47, *243*, 245
Davenport, Philippa 41
deadheading 71–73
Delphinium 32, 37, *76*, 164
  D. 'Molly Buchanan' 37, 144–45, *146*
designing gardens 79, 265
Dianthus barbatus 86, 145, *146*
dill 207, *210*, 227
drought-tolerant plants 264

E
Eastick, Anne 65, 73, 169, 245
Echinacea 86, 235
  E. 'Fatal Attraction' 235, *237*
  E. 'SunSeekers Pomegranate' 86, 235
  E. 'SunSeekers Red' 86, 235
edging plants 79
elephant's foot plant 130
Emorsgate Seeds 37
Erigeron 193
  E. karvinskianus 146, 147, 253
Erysimum cheiri 99, 110–11, *113*
Eucalyptus gunnii 55, 82, 111–12, *113*
Eucryphia 147, *149*
  E. glutinosa 27
  E. × *nymansensis* 147
Euphorbia oblongata 105
  E. wulfenii 264
Exochorda × *macrantha* 'The Bride' 112, *113*
  E. × *m.* 'Lotus Moon' 112

F
Farmer Street 22–25
ferns 34, 112, 114, *115*, 117, 127, 128, 258

Ferula communis 264
flowers, cut 19, 35–37, 79–86, 95, 262
Forsythia 38, 55, 74, 82, 98, 242, 245–46, 247
French beans 207–08, 209
French tarragon 197, 208, 210, 226
Frost, Adam 221

G

Galanthus elwesii 82, 246, 247
   G. e. 'Grumpy' 82, 249
Galium odoratum 114
Garden Museum 62
Gardeners' World 61, 221
garlic 197
   garlic spray 155
gaura 164–65, 166
Gazania 235–36, 237
Geranium 73, 86, 166, 167–68, 193, 195, 196
   G. 'Rozanne' 147–48, 149
Geum 148, 149
Gladiolus 82, 129, 148, 149
glasshouses 52, 212–13
Godfrey, Penny 65, 93, 245, 252
gold-edged winter daphne 243
ground elder 75
Guinness, Bunny 45, 46–47, 51, 55, 65, 120, 129, 169, 253

H

Haemanthus albiflos 130
Hamamelis × *intermedia* 'Pallida' 248, 249
Hambledon Gardening Club 252
hanging baskets 25
Harkness, Philip 30, 188–90
Harkness Roses 30, 187–90
hawthorn 98
Heath, Lady 30, 37, 42, 63
Heath, Sir Barrie 37, 42, 63
hedging 46, 49, 51, 55, 56–57, 69, 86–91, 240, 265
Helleborus (hellebores) 126, 240, 251, 258, 259
   H. 'Angel Glow' 250
   H. niger 61, 83, 86, 250, 257
Henley-on-Thames 45–59, 60, 75, 98, 119, 144, 177, 216, 236
herbs 35–37, 77, 196–227
Hesperantha coccinea 34
Hessayon, D.G. 61
Heuchera 'Plum Pudding' 150, 151
Hillier Garden Centre 38, 63
Hippeastrum 'Apple Blossom' 116, 117
Hiram Walker 15, 29, 39, 51
holly 46, 87
hollyhocks 93
honesty 71, 118, 120, 241
honeysuckle 55, 98, 253, 256

Hopkirk, Jenny 142
Horatio's Garden, National Spinal Injuries Centre 65–67, 66
hornbeam 265
horse chestnut 100–01
Hosta 151–54, 152–53, 250
   H. 'War Paint' 130
houseplants 78–79, 130
Hunnings, Annabel 26, 27–28
Hunnings, Paul 15–16, 22, 24, 29, 38, 39, 51, 55, 179, 187
Hunnings, Tom 22, 26, 27–28, 32, 33, 55, 87
Hunnings, William 26, 27–28, 32, 40, 60–61, 145
Hyacinthus orientalis (hyacinth) 99, 118, 119
Hydrangea 82, 135
   H. arborescens 'Annabelle' 99, 155–57, 156
Hylotelephium cauticola 'Coca-Cola' 157, 158

I

Ilex crenata 87
Iris 105
   I. pallida 264
   I. pseudacorus 34
   I. unguicularis 240
   I. unguicularis 'Mary Barnard' 82, 83, 250, 251, 252
ivy-leaved cyclamen 242, 243, 244

J

Jackson, Miss 20
Japanese anemone 228, 229, 231
Japanese maples 69
Japanese quince 73–74, 82, 106, 108
Jasminum nudiflorum 251, 252

K

Kalette 199, 208, 210, 211

L

lady's mantle 82, 136, 137
lamb's ear 79, 173, 175
lamb's lettuce 219
Laserpitium siler 264
Laskett 51, 88–89, 91
Lathyrus 86, 160
Laurus nobilis 252–53, 254–55
Lavandula (lavender) 19, 264
   L. angustifolia 'Hidcote' 69, 160–61, 162
lawns 78, 263
lemons 108, 109
lettuces 218, 220
Leucojum 118, 120
lilies (*Lilium*) 19, 82, 161, 162

lily of the valley 80–81, 102, 108, 109, 130
Longstock Park Water Garden 33
Lonicera 131
   L. fragrantissima 98, 253, 256
Lunaria annua 'Chedglow' 118, 120

M

McVicar, Jekka 226–27
Magnolia grandiflora 74
   M. g. 'Exmouth' 38, 86, 236, 237
maidenhair 130
Malus × *floribunda* 69
Malvern Spring Festival 62
Mandevilla sanderi 162, 163
marguerite 141, 142
masterwort 141, 142
meadow rue 175, 176
meadows 37–38
melons 210, 211
Mexican fleabane 146, 147, 253
Michaelmas daisies 24, 77–78, 230
micro-herbs 77
mimosa 240, 242, 243
monk's hood 82, 134, 135
mountain totara 131
mustard 'Red Frills' 227

N

Narcissus see daffodils
nasturtiums 214, 215
National Garden Scheme (NGS) 25, 27, 33, 38, 40, 63–67, 135
navelwort 122, 123, 125
Nepeta 73, 160, 162, 163–64
   N. × *faassenii* 32, 164
   N. racemosa 'Walker's Low' 79, 163
Nerine bowdenii 236, 237, 240, 252
Nicholson, Polly 94–95

O

Oenothera lindheimeri 164–65, 166
Omphalodes cappadocica 'All Summer Blues' 122, 123, 125
onions 214, 214
Oven's wattle 240, 242, 243

P

Paeonia 165, 167
   P. lactiflora 'White Wings' 165, 166
Pan Global Plants 242
pansies 105, 132, 258
paper whites 98–99
Parker-Swift, Diana and Stephen 163
Parker's Wholesale 117, 129
parsley 214, 215, 216, 227
Parsons, Roger 160
Patterson, Richard 92
peaches 172, 173

pearlbush 112, *113*
Pelargonium 135, 167–68, 193, 196
    P. 'Attar of Roses' 104
    P. 'Frank Headley' *195*
    P. 'Sweet Mimosa' 86, *166*, 167
Penstemon *166*, 168–69, 240
peony 165, *166*, 167
Peruvian lily 86, 136–40, *138*
Philadelphus 38, 74
    P. 'Petite Perfume Pink' 131
Phlomis 264
Phlox 19
    P. paniculata 'White Admiral' 86, 169, *170*
Photinia × *fraseri* 'Red Robin' 74
Pieris 69
planting 46, 77
Plumbago auriculata 73, 169, *171*
Plumptre, George 63, 65
Podocarpus nivalis 131
ponds *31*, 33–35, *49*, 52, *53*
Pottage, Matthew 109, 127, 130–31, 169
Potts, Chris 151, 154
primroses 14, *15*, 16, 61, 86, *122*, 125
Primula 34
    P. vulgaris 86, *122*, 125
protecting plants 78
pruning 25, 73–75, 189, 192–93, 227
Prunus 'Kursar' 169, 172, *173*
    P. persica 'Peregrine' 172, *173*
    P. × *subhirtella* 'Autumnalis' 169, 172
Pryce, Kevin *5*, 40, *54*, 74, 78, 91, 155, 172, 262
purple top 175, *176*, 177

R

raspberries 74–75, 216–18, *217*
Raven, Sarah 35, 44, 61, 99, 104–05, 111, 126, 180, 211, 233
The Red House *26*, 27–30, 75, 106
Rhinanthus minor 37
RHS Chelsea Flower Show 62, 140, 165, 167
RHS Garden Wisley 62, 103, 110, 127, 130, 172, 258–59
Roads, Dawn 43
rocket 199, 218
Romneya coulteri *238*, 239
Rootgrow 187, 189
Rosa (roses) 18, 30, 46, 68–69, 71, 92, *182*, 183–93
    climbing roses 190–92
    pot-grown vs bare-root 188–89
    pruning 25, 189, 192–93, *254–55*
    R. 'Albertine' 68
    R. 'Alister Stella Gray' 68
    R. 'Chandos Beauty' 30, 71, 86, 132, *184–85*, 187, 188, 190, *191*, 193
    R. 'Compassion' 183, 192

R. 'Crimson Shower' 69
R. 'Duchess of Cornwall' 104
R. 'The Fairy' 30
R. 'Garnette Rose' 30
R. 'The Generous Gardener' 68–69
R. 'Gertrude Jekyll' 192
R. 'Graham Thomas' 86, 190
R. 'Himalayan Musk' 68
R. 'Kiftsgate' 192
R. 'Mary Delany' 68
R. 'New Dawn' 192
R. 'Paul's Himalayan Musk' 86, 192
R. 'Peace' 30
R. 'Rambling Rector' 86, 192
R. 'Rosemary Harkness' 30
rosemary 226, 227

S

sage 86, 172, 174
salad leaves 218–19
Salvia 228, 172
    S. 'Amethyst' 174
    S. 'Amistad' 86, 174
    S. candelabrum 264
    S. farinacea 'Victoria Blue' 86, *173*, 174
    S. nemorosa 'Caradonna' 86, 174
    S. patens 174
Sarcococca confusa 128, *256*, 257, 258, 259
sedum 79, 86, 103, 157
Seseli hippomarathrum 264
shade, plants for 130
shallots 219, *220*
shaving brush plant 130
Shaw, Tony 151
Siberian bugloss 154
Sienna Hosta 151
Sissinghurst 44
slender vervain *176*, 177
Smith, Delia 29
Smith's Garden Centre 62–63, 111, 114
snapdragon *83*, 86, 230, *231*
snowdrops 82, 114, 120, 240, 246, *247*, 249, 262
snowflakes *118*, 120
soil 60, 69, 70
South Lawn 14, 16–20
spearmint 'Tashkent' 226
speedwell *176*, 177
spring 98–131
spring onions 219, *220*
squirrels 95, 263
Stachys byzantina 'Silver Carpet' 79, *173*, 175
staking 77–78
star jasmine 52, 86
Stewart, Katie 41
Stone, Mike 33–34, 35
stonecrop 157

strawberries 219, *220*, 221
Strong, Roy 51, *88–89*, 91
Stuart-Smith, Tom 264–65
summer 132–227
Sutton Place 38
sweet box *256*, 257, 258
sweet peas 16, 86, 105, 132, *159*, 160
sweet william 86, 145, *146*
sweet woodruff 114
Swift, Joe 65
Symphyotrichum 230, 232
    S. novi-belgii 77–78

T

tarragon, French 197, 208, *210*, 226
Taxus 46, 69, 87
Tetley, Penny 52, *53*, 92
Thalictrum 175, *176*
Thompson & Morgan 29, 211
Thorpe, Margaret 38, 73
thyme 197, 221, *222–23*, 225, 226
tips 70–93
Titchmarsh, Alan 52, 61, *64*, 65, 68–69, 218, 225
Toad Hall 62–63
tomatoes *224*, 225
tools and equipment 91–93
topiary *49*, 52, *53*, 86–91
Trachelospermum 223
    T. jasminoides 52, 86
treasure flower 235–36, *237*
tree peonies 165
trees 38, 40, 47, 69, 265
Tulipa (tulips) 82, 94–95, 99, 105, 125–26, 155
    growing 126, 127
    T. 'Angélique' 82, 99, *124*, 125, 129
    T. 'China Town' 82, 126
    T. 'Spring Green' 82, 126
    T. 'White Valley' 104

V

vegetables 35–37, 52–55, 196–227
Verbena bonariensis 175, *176*, 177
    V. rigida *176*, 177
Veronica 79, 103, *176*, 177
    V. rigidula 35, *36*
Viburnum 74
    V. × *bodnantense* 'Dawn' *256*, 257
Viola cornuta 105

W

wallflowers 99, 110–11, *113*, 126, 258
watercress 21
Watercroft 19, 30–44, 60, 63, 78, 92, 98, 119, 144, 154, 164, 177, 190, 236, 239
watering 92
weeds 75
Westray, Annabel 205

White, Claire 38, 61–62
wild garlic 19
windflower 228, *229*, *231*
winter 240–65
winter-flowering honeysuckle 253, *256*
winter jasmine *251*, 252
wisteria 132, 177–80, *178–79*
witch hazel *248*, 249
Woburn Farm Plants 140
Woodbridges Grocery & Bakery 135

Y
yellow flag iris 34
yellow rattle 37
yew 38, 46, *49*, 51, 55, *56–57*, 69, 87–91, 265
Young, Chris 232
Young, Kirsty 61
Young, Lucy 16, 41, 44, 63, 127

Z
zinnia 86, 180, *181*, 183

Picture credits

The publisher would like to thank the following for their kind permission to reproduce their photographs:

(Key: a-above; b-below/bottom; c-centre; f-far; l-left; r-right; t-top)

12 Mary Berry. 15 Mary Berry. 17 Mary Berry. 23 Mary Berry. 26 Mary Berry. Shutterstock.com: Hart / Evening News (b). **31 Mary Berry. 36 Mary Berry. 39 Mary Berry. 46 Bunny Guinness. 48 Mary Berry. 50 Mary Berry. 54 Wolf Rock Media Ltd. 66 Horatio's Garden:** Mark Lord (tl); Mark Lord (tr); Lucy Shergold (b). **64 Val Bourne. 68 BBC Gardeners' World magazine:** Neil Hepworth. **83 GAP Photos:** Elke Borkowski (br); Evgeniya Vlasova - Camellia Park, Locarno (tl); Martin Hughes-Jones (tr); Tim Gainey (bl). **94 Britt Willoughby. 104 Jonathan Buckley. 108 GAP Photos:** Nicola Stocken (tl); Nicola Stocken (br). **113 GAP Photos:** Elke Borkowski (b). **118 GAP Photos:** Jonathan Buckley - Garden: West Dean Gardens (tl); Jason Ingram (bl). **121 GAP Photos:** Visions. **130 RHS:** Lee Charlton. **134 GAP Photos:** Richard Bloom (t). **141 GAP Photos:** Mandy Bradshaw (tr); John Glover (tl); John Glover (br). **143 GAP Photos:** Jonathan Buckley. **146 Blackmore & Langdon:** (tr). **GAP Photos:** Trevor Sima (tl); Visions Premium (bl). **149 GAP Photos:** Mark Bolton (tr); Tim Gainey (br). **158 GAP Photos:** Nova Photo Graphik. **159 GAP Photos:** Annaick Guittery. **162 GAP Photos:** Elke Borkowski (br); Paul Debois (tl); Ernie Janes (bl). **166 GAP Photos:** Pernilla Bergdahl (tr). **170 GAP Photos:** Liz Every. **173 GAP Photos:** Mark Bolton (br); Martin Hughes-Jones (tl). **176 Alamy Stock Photo:** Zena Elea (bl); Magdalena Iordache (br). **GAP Photos:** Jacqui Dracup (tr); Jason Ingram (tl). **178 Mary Berry. 179 Mary Berry. 184–185 Mary Berry. 188 Harkness Rose Company. 194 Mary Berry. 203 GAP Photos:** Fiona Lea (br). **206 GAP Photos:** Chris Burrows (br); Visions (t). **210 GAP Photos:** Jonathan Buckley - Charles Dowding's No Dig Garden, Somerset (tl); Martin Hughes-Jones (tr); Jonathan Buckley (bl); Sine Lewis (br). **215 Alamy Stock Photo:** Clare Gainey (bl). **GAP Photos:** Tim Gainey (t); Visions (br). **220 GAP Photos:** Martin Hughes-Jones (bl); Gary Smith (tr); Maddie Thornhill (br). **226 Jason Ingram. 229 GAP Photos:** Tim Gainey. **231 GAP Photos:** Claire Gainey (tl); Tim Gainey (tr); Howard Rice (br). **234 GAP Photos:** Elke Borkowski. **237 GAP Photos:** Martin Hughes-Jones (tr); Adrian James (tl). **Clive Nichols:** The Old Rectory, Haselbech, Northamptonshire (br). **238 Clive Nichols:** Alderwood House, Kent. **241 GAP Photos:** John Glover. **243 GAP Photos:** Jaqcui Dracup (tr); Martin Hughes-Jones (tl); Howard Rice (bl). **247 GAP Photos:** Mandy Bradshaw (b); Marina Walker (t). **248 GAP Photos:** Jacqui Dracup. **251 GAP Photos:** Howard Rice (bl); Dave Zubraski (br). **256 GAP Photos:** Jonathan Buckley (tl); Jonathan Buckley (tr); Howard Rice - Garden: Cambridge Botanic Gardens (bl). **264 Eva Nemeth**.

Acknowledgements

Mary's acknowledgements

Many thank yous...

This book is all about my love of gardening. I have no training, I have a blank spot for the Latin names, but I have a passion for the great outdoors and the joy that a garden gives. It has been a great learning experience, with many mistakes and lots of lessons learnt. I have had everything from a humble backyard to 3.5 acres in my time. I am now down to something much more manageable, having started from scratch six years ago.

To my publishers – thank you to Chris Young and Ruth O'Rourke for commissioning this book. It is a true passion of mine and thank you to them for taking the plunge. To Maxine Pedliham, for the design and creativity of the book, and to all the team at DK.

A big thank you to Juliet Roberts for the monthly visits and putting my thoughts and parables to paper, writing in seasons made the most sense and guides you through the year. Thank you for your understanding of my non-gardening terms and for recording my experiences, which I hope will help others. A sheer pleasure to work with.

Britt Willoughby, our photographer, thank you for these magical photographs and the early rises to get the atmospheric photos and sunlight gleaming, I am delighted. Thank you to Peter Borcherds of Wolf Rock Media Ltd for the inspiring overhead drone photography.

I asked some gardening experts, who I respect enormously, to share their expertise, and they have been kind enough to donate their wisdom to the book.

To the home team – Kevin Pryce, our gardener of 32 years and who this book is dedicated to, thank you for saying 'no problem' to anything I suggest, even on a wet winter's day! You are the best, I look forward to every Thursday morning at 7:30am! Lucy Young, 36 years by my side, keeping me on the straight and narrow, so strange not to be talking recipes!

And to my husband, Paul, for his years of deadheading and giving me free rein on the design and creation of our gardens over the years – how special it is to share them together with a glass of wine on a summer's day.

Publisher's acknowledgements

DK would like to thank Lucy Young and all of Mary's team for their help and support, Jo Penfold for hair and make-up, Kathy Steer for proofreading, Vanessa Bird for indexing, Adam Brackenbury and Tom Morse for repro work, Mark Clifton for the garden plan, and Jordan Lambley for design assistance.

Resources

Here are some of my favourite suppliers and sources of inspiration:

Claire Austin
claireaustin-hardyplants.co.uk

Crocus *crocus.co.uk*

Gardeners' World *gardenersworld.com*

Harkness Roses *roses.co.uk*

National Garden Scheme *ngs.org.uk*

Roger Parsons Sweet Peas
englishsweetpeas.co.uk

Royal Horticultural Society *rhs.org.uk*

Sarah Raven *sarahraven.com*

Editorial Director Ruth O'Rourke
Art Director Maxine Pedliham
Gardening Design Manager Barbara Zuniga
Senior Editor Alastair Laing
Senior Production Editor Tony Phipps
Senior Production Controller Stephanie McConnell
Publishing Director Stephanie Jackson

Editorial Juliet Roberts, Dawn Titmus
Design Vicky Read
Photography Britt Willoughby
Consultant Gardening Publisher Chris Young

First published in Great Britain in 2026 by
Dorling Kindersley Limited
20 Vauxhall Bridge Road,
London SW1V 2SA

The authorised representative in the EEA is
Dorling Kindersley Verlag GmbH. Arnulfstr. 124,
80636 Munich, Germany

Copyright © Mary Berry 2026
Copyright © 2026 Dorling Kindersley Limited
A Penguin Random House Company
10 9 8 7 6 5 4 3 2 1
001–345883–Feb/2026

All rights reserved.
No part of this publication may be reproduced, stored in or introduced into a retrieval system, or transmitted, in any form, or by any means (electronic, mechanical, photocopying, recording, or otherwise), without the prior written permission of the copyright owner.

No part of this publication may be used or reproduced in any manner for the purpose of training artificial intelligence technologies or systems. In accordance with Article 4(3) of the DSM Directive 2019/790, DK expressly reserves this work from the text and data mining exception.

A CIP catalogue record for this book
is available from the British Library.
ISBN: 978-0-2417-2665-5

Printed and bound in China

www.dk.com

This book was made with Forest Stewardship Council™ certified paper – one small step in DK's commitment to a sustainable future. Learn more at www.dk.com/uk/information/sustainability